Advance Praise for WIN! The Hispanic Market

Isabel continues to be the leading expert in understanding how to win Hispanic consumers for life. She has continually challenged us to elevate our insights, marketing capabilities, and resources to fully capture the loyalty of our future consumers. We are grateful for her intellect and passion.

John Compton, CEO
PepsiCo Americas Global Foods and Snacks Group

Success in business today requires not just understanding the potential of the Hispanic market, but its complexity as well. Isabel Valdés has brought together **nearly 20 Hispanic marketing experts to lay out a clear and cogent blueprint for successfully penetrating this market** and debunking the old stereotypes about Hispanics. This new collaborative work brings a modern awareness to the concepts of language, acculturation, technology, media, engagement, and targeting. **Another must read.**

Monica Lozano
CEO, ImpreMedia

Isabel's new book is **a provocative invitation to a new conversation on the Hispanic market.** America is becoming multicultural and Hispanics are leading the way. But this is no longer a Spanish-only group. It is increasingly bicultural and bilingual and their attitudes, behaviors, and beliefs will need to be deeply understood in order co capture the opportunity of the new mainstream. It is the reality of youth today and is the future of the nation.

Antonio Lucio, Chief Marketing, Strategy and Corporate
Development Officer, Visa Inc.

The leadership in the C-Suite must read *WIN The Hispanic Market* and ask executives responsible for marketing, advertising, sales, retail and consumer insights to instigate action within their respective areas of responsibility. The book provides definite and solid intelligence to build the business case and the tools to size the opportunity to invest in the Hispanic market. The expertise and insights shared by the contributors is equivalent to going to advanced executive training in the Ivy League, with the best in the industry sharing the latest tools and know-how to successfully target this lucrative market segment, in a friendly format.

Orlando Padilla, President & CEO
Padilla NetWorks LLC; Former Director, Global Public Policy
Center, General Motors Corporation

Brilliant! Isabel has collected a data-driven and context-rich analysis of the Hispanic market, which is not only relevant today but will help leaders committed to growth identify one of the world's biggest markets here in the U.S. **A must-read for corporate leaders and entrepreneurs, to managers and employees** aspiring to understand and "Win the Hispanic market."

Manuel Gonzalez, Chief Executive Officer
National Society of Hispanic MBAs

Win the Hispanic Market by Hispanic marketing and marketing research pioneer M. Isabel Valdés and her colleagues provide **progressive insights what American corporations must do in order to assure their success with Hispanic consumers and their community.** To understand the Hispanic/Latino community and its complexities requires knowledge, engagement, and investment. Growing brand loyalty and product consumption only occurs when business understands the consumer and has a responsive and qualified labor force; the Hispanic/Latino market is no exception.

> Douglas X. Patiño, PhD, Vice Chancellor Emeritus
> California State University System;
> Former Secretary, California Health and Welfare Agency

Once again, we applaud Isabel Valdes for her tireless contributions to Hispanic market knowledge. This time, she brought together the best and brightest experts in our field. The result is **a superb compendium of valuable insights and tools that marketing practitioners can use for winning in the Hispanic century.** These insights and tools range from highly persuasive approaches for measuring ROI of Hispanic market investments to practical approaches for geo-demographic targeting of Hispanic consumers. It's a must read for those already committed to the Hispanic market as well as for those that still need evidence of its value.

> Carlos Arce, Managing Partner
> ArceZmud, LLC; Chief Scientist, EthniFacts, Inc.

Isabel and her team of experts provide the keys to the vault by **delivering smart and strategic advice for marketing to U.S. Hispanics.** This is the best book Isabel has written!!

> Tom Maney, Senior Vice President/Advertising Sales
> Fox Hispanic Media

Where is your organization's growth coming from? Where will your growth come from in the next five, ten, or twenty years? With Hispanics accounting for nearly half of U.S. consumer spending growth and over half of U.S. population growth it is paramount to win the Hispanic market. . . . *WIN! The Hispanic Market* provides **unique and valuable insights to help your organization win the present and the future.**

> Pablo Schneider, President
> Corporate Creations International, Inc.

Isabel Valdés is by far the most prolific researcher and author on Hispanic marketing of our time. Her latest book helps us understand how to "win with Hispanics in the long run," and takes a multidisciplinary approach—across diversity practices, marketing strategy, research, and so much more. **This book is a must-read for those interested in seeing their business grow.** It will become the basis for developing a company's winning strategies for Hispanics.

> Jake Beniflah, PhD, Executive Director
> The Center for Multicultural Science, San Francisco

WIN!

THE HISPANIC MARKET

Strategies for
Business Growth

M. Isabel Valdés

CONTRIBUTORS

Steve Moya • Carlos Orta • Michael Klein & David Wellisch

Alison K. Paul • Carlos Santiago • Jessica Pantanini • Marie Quintana

Gabriela Alcántara-Diaz • Don Longo • César Melgoza

Doug Darfield • Roberto Orci • Lee Vann • Lucia Ballas-Traynor

Martha Montoya • Federico Subervi • Carlos Garcia • Derene Allen

Paramount Market Publishing, Inc.

Paramount Market Publishing, Inc.
950 Danby Road, Suite 136
Ithaca, NY 14850
www.paramountbooks.com
Voice: 607-275-8100; 888-787-8100
Fax: 607-275-8101

Publisher: James Madden
Editorial Director: Doris Walsh

Library of Congress Catalog Number:
Cataloging in Publication Data available
ISBN 10: 0-9830436-8-X
ISBN 13: 978-0-9830436-8-3

The greatest benefit of diversity in business is not merely that it makes us more inclusive, it's that it collectively makes us stronger. It draws together different skills and talents. In fact, success in the marketplace depends on our ability to recognize and reflect the diversity of each community we serve.

Increasingly, the Latino community, with its explosive population growth, its high cultural prevalence and its spending power, is a group we must intimately understand. Harnessing its growth potential is the key to success for any enterprise in the world today. By promoting and celebrating this rich culture in our own companies, we add to our skills and insights, and ultimately, deliver better results.

In the words of the great Mexican writer Octavio Paz, "What sets worlds in motion is the interplay of differences."

— INDRA NOOYI
CHAIRMAN & CEO, PEPSICO
PURCHASE, N.Y.
DECEMBER 2, 2011

Contents

When the Future Meets Today

Steve Moya

ACHIEVING real and sustainable growth is today's business issue. It frames the daily challenge in boardrooms and C-Suites.

It would be an oversimplification to argue that this has always been the case. Never before have companies faced such unpredictable consumers—with far ranging and erratic tastes and interests, operating in such uncertain economic times. Never has ubiquitous technology empowered consumers with the information and buying leverage that currently exists.

Never before have companies faced the onslaught of competitors, some morphing within an industry and others entering from seemingly unrelated sectors. There are many additional factors that make attaining real (not short-sighted, add-on costs, which consumers put up with but dislike) and sustainable growth (brands that cover so much of what consumers want and need that they have no reason to look elsewhere), all creating a much more challenging endeavor for today's business leaders.

It is this environment that should compel us to draw on the wisdom of Peter Drucker who talked about "the future that's already happened." With that phrase he was saying that there are clear signs that new directions are in place even if others don't see them. He believed those instances present a significant business opportunity because many competitors will timidly wait for all the evidence to come in to validate a shift. By that time, the competitive opportunity is gone.

The future is here

In many ways, the U.S. Hispanic market is "the future that's already happened."

Scale Hispanics are projected to comprise one of five Americans by 2020. Although that is distant for marketers worried about the pressures of today, it is directionally important.

Growth Hispanic population compound annual growth rate (CAGR) between 2000 and 2010 was 3.6 percent versus 0.5 percent among non-Hispanics.

Maturity While Hispanics represent America's youngest ethnicity with 55 percent younger than age 30, the fastest growing Hispanic segment is adults aged 45 to 64 (6.3 percent CAGR 2000–2010).

Income Though starting from a lower base, 40 percent of Hispanic households now earn over $50,000 (even in years when overall household wealth diminished).

Buying power Hispanic percentage of overall buying power is expected to continue to grow while non-Hispanics' buying power shrinks. From 2000 to 2010, Hispanic buying power grew at 7.8 percent annually (CAGR), twice the rate of non-Hispanics.

So if growth is the issue, and Hispanics are growing as a share of the population and earning more, the response would be pretty simple, right? Yes and No. Yes, because the opportunity is not only here now, but also the math points to greater opportunity ahead. No, because targeting this segment appears challenging to many, in some cases leading to marginal efforts or total avoidance.

In the spirit of support, and as someone with experience in the General Market and Hispanic space, I offer the following thoughts to businesses and the corporate world, in particular.

Embrace a macro understanding of the changing American marketplace: Hail the New America!

The country looks different today compared with just 30 years ago. As we know, the first Baby Boomers filled out their Medicare paperwork in

2011; a true sign of an aging population. Today, the elderly are White and the young are Hispanic, African-American, Asian, or multi-ethnic. Culturally, the population covers the acculturation spectrum and, while U.S.-born Hispanics now drive Hispanic growth, tipping the scale towards the more acculturated, they remain Hispanic at the core. The impact of these shifts will be felt for years to come.

Understand the reset. Many have come to recognize that the 2007 downturn was more than another recession, with resulting cyclical adjustments. Long-lasting structural changes appear real and they will impact the economy, society, and individuals long-term. The greatest challenge will be the labor market and our ability to meet job demand. This is a global issue affecting both established and emerging markets. In the U.S. we already see changes in purchasing, housing arrangements, saving rates, a new level of "sharing," and more. It's a new environment and marketers must learn to navigate under these conditions.

Follow the Ten States. In America, ten states have 50 percent of the population. More importantly, these ten states are also responsible for a disproportionate share of the economy, electoral votes, and cultural influence. They are also the most ethnically diverse, affecting not only those states, but the remaining 40 states of the nation. Marketers must understand this dynamic and acknowledge it in strategic and tactical planning. For example, billboards in the ten may increasingly shift toward visuals over words, to reach all populations regardless of language use. How to allocate dollars to the ten versus the forty will also be up for discussion.

Organize to address the changing marketplace

Hire people who can think globally. This nation of 300+ million is a microcosm of the world and should be approached that way. Traditional marketers are increasingly irrelevant.

Reframe the question. It isn't *how do you market?* It's *how do you grow?* Marketing executives can't continue to wait at the back end of the process. They need to be part of early decision making on what consumers want and need, and then how to communicate the value you offer.

End the ghetto. If smart segmentation becomes a standard for achieving growth, the underfunded and underappreciated ethnic, gender, and generational segments will thrive in corporate America and so will those who drive their programs.

Blend. Make it possible to integrate General Market and segment market strategies and tactics, so that synergies are created and marketers on each side have a stake in total success.

Raise the bar. Segment and general marketers alike must increasingly be challenged and allowed to deliver insights and marketing rigor. Then they must be accountable to deliver growth.

Find external partners who understand their segments and your world: End the mystification

Too often Hispanic marketers and agencies overcomplicate their role and the market they target. This doesn't serve clients in the short run and the marketers in the long run. Guide by simplifying.

Burst the bubble. Many Hispanics live, speak, and think in ways somewhat different than the General Market, but they interact with society as well. They don't live in a bubble and shouldn't be portrayed by agencies that way.

Integrate marketing efforts. Broad marketing will win every time. Advertising should always be employed in conjunction with other elements of the marketing mix, such as direct efforts, community interaction, public relations, cause-related programs, and more.

Hire people who also care. Those who target Hispanics in commercial ways should also contribute to the community's welfare. Corporations need to find alignment by investing in the community and hiring those who do so as well. It's just that simple.

There is a role for corporations and the Hispanic marketing sector in support of the national Hispanic community and it can make a substantial impact on this nation.

Significant Hispanic growth has taken place only since 1980, so generational progress is still in its relative infancy. But if Hispanics are to play a critical role in this prosperous but aging nation, education and skill progress must accelerate. Only through innovative new approaches can Hispanics achieve what they need and society requires. There are positive signs that the same innovative thinking seen in business is being applied to local Hispanic community development. We encourage businesses to maintain this direction and momentum.

In closing

The long-term growth projections for the Hispanic market are as robust as they've been since 1980. But marketing in the United States rarely takes the long-view, and in this case it shouldn't.

As I said in the beginning, the future has already happened. So it's critical to understand that the market covered in this book is real today.

Yet, some companies will want more analysis. Some will conclude that in 30 years no one will really be speaking Spanish. Others will assume that total assimilation will kick-in, like they've always theorized. And others will decide that their plate is simply too full.

There is a great deal to be learned from the authors who have contributed their expertise to this book and I hope you take full advantage.

Steve Moya is senior adviser at Santiago Solutions Group.

Business Growth and Sustainability Are Hispanic!

M. Isabel Valdés
President, IVC In-Culture Marketing

IF THE U. S. Census Bureau is right, and it usually is, by 2040, 51 percent of the total population of the U.S. will be multi-cultural, of these, 56 percent will be Hispanic. From a marketing perspective, a large percentage of these consumers are already here. Right now, 50.1 percent of U.S. children aged three and under, are non-White and that doesn't include babies in Puerto Rico. These young multi-cultural consumers have already joined the marketplace. Together with their pre-teen, teen, and young adult siblings, they are not only developing their product preferences, but they are also using traditional and social media programs, choosing their music and entertainment outlets, their favorite sports, and so on.

In other words, the 2040 "future" multi-cultural customer, patient, client, home buyer, new mom, loan applicant, student, business market is already here, building loyalties, preferences, and consuming. The Hispanic consumer over-indexes exponentially in the young consumer age segments, and therefore, will also be significantly over-represented by 2040, when the total Hispanic population is projected to reach 108 million compared with African Americans at 50 million and Asians, at 31 million. Combined, Hispanics, African Americans, and Asians, add up to 213 million. The mostly White, non-Hispanic, aging, retired baby boomer population will be composed of 205 million people, who are expected to be significantly less active in the marketplace due to age.

As we know, consumers begin to acquire their likes and dislikes at an early age, mostly through their parents, siblings, peers, family friends, and grandparents—in other words, though their cultural communities, which I have labeled "in-culture" for lack of a better term. It follows simple math and logic that every business in America that expects to be successful and thriving in 2040 has to invest to appeal to and win these consumers and their families.

Otherwise, why or how will they build deep and lasting "emotional connections" with your brand? Why would these consumers purchase your brand, or go to your bank or visit your clinic or hospital, attend your college or university, if you are not a part of their personal network and cultural community? If you are not close, inviting, and talking to them, in a cultural language that is meaningful and resonates with them? Why would they spontaneously start consuming your brand of beverage, or patronize your restaurant, go to your bank, or hospital if you don't invite them—or their parents or grandparents—in?

Is your corporation investing in the opportunity?

What is surprising is that the majority of U.S. corporations ignore the $1.1 trillion U.S. Hispanic consumer market. As global CEO "Sol" Trujillo said at the Wall Street Summit in New York in October 2011, "The U.S. Hispanic market will soon be the eleventh largest economy in the world," if it were a separate country. That puts the U.S. Hispanic market in the same category as Brazil, Russia, India, and China (the BRIC countries), with more per capita purchasing power than many of the G-20 member nations as well.[1] In other words, the U.S. Hispanic market has the potential to be the main source of growth for most business categories in a slow economy, but only a small number of corporations invest well and accordingly, attract and invite these consumers with relevant products, services, and messages, using the best in-culture, professional expertise that is available right now.

A 2011 study by AHAA[2] (Association of Hispanic Advertising

---

1. Pablo Schneider quoted "Sol" Trujillo on *Fox News Latino*, October 28, 2011.
   http://latino.foxnews.com/latino/politics/2011/10/28/follow-money-it-leads-to-latino-market

2. "Advertising 2011 Budget Alignment: Maximizing Impact in the Hispanic Market," *2011 AHAA Hispanic Advertising Ad Trend, Full Report*, by Carlos Santiago, CEO, SSG and Cristina Garcia, PhD, Statistics Professor, USC; commissioned by AHAA

Agencies) found that only 27 companies—5 percent of the top 500 advertisers—had an aggregate Hispanic advertising expenditure of just over 14 percent, comparable to the percentage of adults that are Hispanic according to the 2010 Census. This makes no sense, particularly when it has been demonstrated that strategic, sustained, and robust investment in the Hispanic market not only provides growth and sustainability to those corporations but also increases shareholder value.[3] "With a confidence level over 95 percent a best-in-class company allocating one quarter of its ad spend to Hispanic media (Spanish and Bilingual) over five years would generate annual revenue growth of 6.7 percent," according to the AHAA study, which includes only advertising, "over-the-line" expenditures.

A few best-in-class companies are already experiencing steady growth from their Hispanic market investment. However, based on this same study, we know that 57 percent of these top 500 advertisers "Don't get it" and spent less than one percent targeting the Hispanic consumer market in 2010. Many in the trade question this lack of investment.

A business blind spot?

The social implications of this colossal demographic shift and exponential Hispanic population growth are obvious and explicit as well as subtle and even subconscious. The obvious is that America is becoming brown and black, and that mainstream American culture is shifting. We are no longer surprised by learning that the most popular sauce in America is a Mexican-style *salsa picante*, or that one of the best-loved ice cream flavors is Dulce de Leche, or that every day there are growing numbers of multicultural icons among artists and musicians, media programs, fashion leaders and so on.

However, there are the unconscious responses—those we may not be aware of or that are not verbalized. I believe the latter may account for some of the reticence to seriously target the Hispanic market. This blind spot can have negative implications when it comes to business decision-making.

3. "Does a Well-Resourced Hispanic Corporate Strategy Translate into Shareholder Value Creation?" by Santiago Solutions Group, Inc., 2006.

Let me borrow from Malcolm Gladwell, the bestselling author of *The Tipping Point* and *Blink*. In *Blink*, Gladwell talks about "thin slicing," that fast, unconscious psychological response mechanism that "makes us" make subconcious decisions based on preconceived, erroneous ideas. I wonder if this could be the case with Hispanic marketing.

In my more than three decades in the Hispanic marketing field, first as a graduate student researcher at Stanford's Institute for Communications Research, and later as the founder and CEO of Hispanic Market Connections, Inc.[4] and still later as an Hispanic marketing consultant and strategist, I have had opportunities to interact with hundreds of clients and observe how they perceive the Hispanic market. In an infamous case that I included in my first book (*Hispanic Market Handbook*, Gale Research, Inc., 1995), a marketing executive at a car manufacturing company in Detroit told me back then, that marketing cars to Hispanics had no purpose, "Big Sombrero, No Money." Unfortunately, a stereotype that has been proven wrong many times continues to live in the unconscious mind of American popular culture. "Hispanics don't have money." Never mind that every 12 months or so, the Hispanic market "creates" another $75 billion to $100 billion in disposable income.

Hispanic Marketing "Sustainability"
Projected growth _every 12 months_

- 2.1 million **new** Hispanic consumers, about 5,000 a day, contributed mostly by higher fertility rates (2.4 births per Latina vs. 1.8 for White non-Hispanic) and less by immigration
- $75 to $100 billion **more** in income
- Half a million **new** Hispanic households
- $1.1 trillion in estimated spending power in 2011

Fortunately, not every business succumbs to stereotypes. For example, in the late 1990s, Honda retained me to team up with its Hispanic advertising agency, La Agencia de Orci and Asociados, to introduce its brand to the Hispanic market. The directive from the Japanese CEO was clear: "Win the Hispanic market not once, but long-term" and "earn the right to do business with the Hispanic community." He suggested that I take a month to think about and propose a

---

4. Hispanic Market Connections, Inc., was sold and publicly traded in 1998.

comprehensive strategic primary research program that would provide the insights and intelligence to win the market. He added, "It does not matter the color of the hand holding the dollar, but to be able to earn it with respect!" The funds allocated to "win the Hispanic market" were commensurate with the opportunity, and with the savvy expertise of the folks at La Agencia, in less than a year Honda's sedan models were the best selling among Hispanics for decades.[5] It was done "in-culture" building "Shares of Heart."

In addition, we rarely learn about the amazing things taking place every day in our community. For example, the story of probably the youngest CEO in America, nine-year-old, Max Valdez, President, Cupcakes to the MAX, who successfully sells cupcakes on a daily basis. It helps to be the son of Jeff Valdez, accomplished Latino film director. However, Max runs the company and it was his idea! Another great story is that of a successful marketer at Frito-Lay, my dear friend Richard Montanez, famous for creating and bringing to market the first line of authentic Hispanic-flavored chips which include the delicious Flamin' Hot Cheetos. He also launched the first bilingual packaging.

Richard proudly tells me that he started his career at Frito-Lay as a janitor's room clerk. He laughs, and adds, "This is the equivalent, the Hispanic version of starting as a clerk in the 'mail room' for the Anglos!"

Who is Hispanic in the U.S.?

Hispanics are considered an ethnic category rather than a racial group. Therefore Hispanics can be from any race—Black, White, Asian, Meztizo Indian, etc.—and are from many cultural backgrounds. Often the uniting factor is the Spanish language and Hispanic culture. In this book, you will find the terms Latino and Hispanic used interchangeably.

Because Hispanics may be of any race, the Census Bureau usually refers to the General Market, "non-Hispanic Whites"—people who have said they are White, but have not indicated they are Hispanic. Three out of every five Hispanics living in the United States were born here.

As Malcolm Gladwell writes in *Blink*, "The giant computer that is our unconscious silently crunches all the data it can from the experiences

---

5. The Honda case study appears in my book, *Marketing to American Latinos: A Guide to the In-culture Approach* (Paramount Market Publishing, Inc., 2000)

we've had, the people we've met, the lessons we've learned, the books we've read, the movies we've seen, and so on, and it forms an opinion. That's what is coming out in the IAT [implicity association test]."[6]

Hence, this book, *Win the Hispanic Market*. To provide the best-in-class from the experts as to why—and how—corporate America must move to successfully do business with the Hispanic consumer market. And it must move quickly.

How many are you missing?

Few companies know how many Hispanics could be their customers and few know how to find out how many of their potential customers are missing. My question is, can you afford not to know the size of the prize?

Good insights can be expensive and require the time and help of experts who know the culture and language of potential and current customers. However, this is "your value business growth, sustainability market segment." This is the consumer segment that adds half a million new households every 12 months, households in the family formation years, and with larger families. This is the market you can go to today when business is slow. But to see reliable results, you want to add value to your research when you turn to experts.

Yet, most corporations have to do "numbers patchwork" to get to some estimated "sort of" reliable Hispanic market business sizing number. When it comes to metrics and tracking results, many overlook a substantial part of their customer base. Sadly, much of the current syndicated data available is incomplete or under-represents Hispanic consumer sales, or is missing culturally relevant facts. Hispanic marketing executives and their teams work hard to target Hispanic consumers. Yet, every time retail data misses a sale or the service delivery of an Hispanic customer, it is counted as a non-Hispanic sale. I call this "the leaky bucket syndrome." In other words, it is almost impossible to get to the true sales numbers, and therefore difficult for managers to ask for, or defend, the appropriate budget allocations. This is a serious flaw in the Hispanic research trade

---

6. *Blink*, Malcolm Gladwell, Back Bay Books, 2007, p. 85.

and, as many authors in this book underscore, it urgently needs to be addressed and solved.

Retailers, marketers, brand managers, not-for-profits, all need a reliable and consistent process for collecting data rather than doing it on a random basis when someone on the board of directors or in the C-Suite asks a question. It must be a base component in the corporate organization. And the process needs to include sharing the data with the people in marketing, finance, product development, sales, and retail to help make grounded, fact-based decisions and avoid missing an important part of your customer base. You should ask these questions and demand reliable answers from your research suppliers, because business growth and sustainability in the foreseeable future requires that you understand deeply the Hispanic market by its metrics.

Live in the present, not the past

In many ways, there is a paradigm shift between the old and new as we complete the first decade of a new century.

In the past, you didn't know how to identify your specific Hispanic customer segments. Thanks to new technology you can now identify Hispanics by country of origin, language and acculturation and learn exactly where they live and the products they purchase. You can see where growth is occurring, and segment the Hispanic market by consumer behavior.

In the past, you assumed that in all high-end business categories, Hispanic customers would respond to advertising in English because you also assumed that Spanish-dominant customers did not have enough money to acquire your products. Now you know that you have Hispanic customers with the necessary income. However, they may not speak or grasp the English language enough to get your advertising message.

In the past, you could not know the language preference of your Hispanic customers. Today you can readily segment Hispanics by language preference and by where they live and shop. Today you also know that many Hispanic consumers who are bilingual prefer to consume media in Spanish because it is part of their cultural heritage, and you know this can be even more effective, since for bilingual consumers, advertising message recall is greater in their primary language.

In the past, you planned products and advertising for the "mainstream," meaning White, English-speaking consumers. The new mainstream is multicultural.

In the past, you could target your Hispanic marketing efforts to a very few states and metro areas and you would reach the majority of Hispanics. Now, Hispanics are dispersing to more markets throughout the United States. New census data and new geo-segmentation technology will help you target more successfully, wherever they are.

In the past, you could target Hispanic consumers successfully mostly or exclusively through mass media. Today you know it is imperative that your corporate platform also include programs reaching the Hispanic community through grassroots organizations, as well as communications programs with the broader Hispanic society, including Hispanic leaders, government and policy makers, with independent PR campaigns directed to them.

In the past, the "digital divide," was huge and Latinos were significantly absent from the internet. Today, Hispanic youth is one of the most active segments in the new electronic social media and you need to include it in your media plan.

In the past, you didn't need to worry about having a multicultural workforce. Now you know that your employees as well as your customers like to see people "who look like them" and reflect the make-up of the United States in their board rooms and C-Suites and at all levels in management. Now, your business growth may depend on the vision, contributions and innovations made by an associate that understands well the multicultural customer.

In the past, you thought you could do without specialized marketers who know and understand Hispanic culture and Hispanic customers. Now, you must incorporate Latino marketers and advertisers into your corporate strategy.

In the past, Hispanic voters were treated as a monolithic group, but Hispanics can no longer be considered as a voting block. Not all Hispanics care about the same issues.

In the past, businesses designed their pay, working hours, benefits, and travel requirements around the needs of White, male-dominated breadwinners. Increasingly the needs of multicultural, two-earner households and single-parent households need to be taken into consideration, which may mean flexible working hours, using technology to hold meetings rather than requiring travel, and childcare or cafeteria benefits, among other things.

In the past, the CEO was boss. Today the consumer is Boss. As former Chairman and CEO of Procter & Gamble, A.G. Lafley says, "Our goal at P&G is to delight our customers at 'two moments of truth': first, when they buy a product, and second, when they use it. To achieve that, we live with our consumers and see the world and opportunities for new product initiatives through their eyes. We do this because we win when more consumers purchase and use our brands—and do so repeatedly."[7] This is the only way to succeed In-culture and build lasting "Heart Shares" with your customers and consumers.

In the past, Hispanic marketing was a choice a few leaders made. Now a holistic and consistent Hispanic strategy is a requirement for innovation and sustainable business growth.

Corporate America and all organizations must respond to this new paradigm by incorporating Hispanics, African Americans, Asians and other cultural groups into their company cultures, from the boardroom

---

7. *The Game Changer: How You Can Drive Revenue and Profit Growth with Innovation,* New York: Crown Business, 2008, pp 4–5.

to product innovation, from retail to basic marketing and advertising. Recognizing the financial power and the growing strength of the multicultural consumer you will be able to respond to the shifts in American society and hence, win in the marketplace.

The Mission — The Book

The mission of this book is to bring together expertise across disciplines that can help you strategize, aim, successfully execute and measure the size of the prize—the sustainable business growth you can expect from the growing Hispanic market.

Certainly one book cannot cover all the possible issues or categories relevant to Hispanic marketing and the marketplace. The book does however bring together Hispanic market experts covering the shared "why" and "how" that apply across corporations and most business categories.

First, the perspective from the board room and Corporate, or C-Suite, Michael Klein and David Wellisch co-founders of Latinum Network (Chapter 1) will tell you why Wall Street will look at and consider your corporate Hispanic strategy in its valuations, and two POVs (Point of View) about why Hispanic representation is needed not only at executive levels of leadership and management but across levels from Carlos Orta and Alison Kenney Paul.

In Chapter 2, Carlos Santiago, CEO of SSG will deep dive into marketing and ask you the questions you need to consider to show you how to right-size the Hispanic business opportunity to avoid disappointment. This section includes a POV regarding the challenges facing the Hispanic market industry.

Throughout the book you will hear from the different experts why you should elevate the Hispanic market in your corporate strategy. As Marie Quintana of PepsiCo tells us in Chapter 3, this is no longer a *niche* market, it is **THE** market, and building deep relationships with retailers is the way to go! Gabriela Alcántara-Diaz shows us how the demographic shifts have impacted the new marketplace even within the Hispanic market and a POV on authentic Hispanic Supermarkets from one of the foremost experts in the industry, Don Longo, closes this retail section.

Chapter 4 focuses on state-of-the-art tools and consumer intelligence. From César Melgoza, CEO of Geoscape, you will learn about the latest in geo-segmentation systems that are helping successful marketers, media planners and retailers today to reach their multi-cultural consumers with laser precision. Also in Chapter 4, you will have access to the best, gold-standard data in language segmentation, media usage and other relevant in-culture socio-demographics from Doug Darfield, Nielsen Media.

In Chapter 5, Roberto Orci, CEO of Acento Advertising, will explain how to make the best choices for reaching your Latino customers, from acculturated to non-acculturated with a comprehensive media plan strategy. Then, Lee Vann, CEO of The Captura Group, shares the know-how on the successful use of a variety of new social media platforms highly popular with Latinos and Lucia Ballas-Traynor, co-founder of CafeMom, shares the latest insights on capturing Latinas online. Closing the chapter is a POV on the oldest Hispanic advertising media, print by business leader Martha Montoya.

In Chapter 6, dedicated to primary Hispanic marketing research, you will find specific steps you need to take to avoid mistakes and limitations with your market data online and not online, by one of the authorities in the industry, Carlos Garcia, SVP of Knowledge Networks and Cada Cabeza online panel. You will also learn the common pitfalls in primary research and what you need to know to make sure your Hispanic marketing research dollars give you the data and reliablility you need, co-authored by Dr. Federico Subervi, Director of the Center for the Study of Latino Media and Markets School of Journalism & Mass Communication, Texas State University-San Marcos and myself. And in Chapter 7, Derene Allen will share her findings regarding why giving back to the community helps you deepen your relationship with your customers.

From the board room to the Hispanic retailer, it is a new game to win the U.S. Hispanic market.

chapter 1

The Boardroom Perspective

Why Wall Street Will Look at Your Hispanic Strategy

Michael Klein and David Wellisch
Co-Founders and Managing Partners, Latinum Network

Memo from the CEO: Grow!
Time to jumpstart growth

It's time for American companies to get growing again. It's never *not* a good time for growth, but the recession, and its impact on household income, has kept many companies in a holding pattern for several years. Other companies have been struggling for reasons related more to strategic or operational factors. Still others, a declining number, have managed to maintain consistent growth through recent market cycles but need to sustain that going forward. For all companies, jumpstarting or maintaining growth is no small task in today's economic environment, with nervous capital markets and mounting government debt, not to mention a consumer economy in the U.S. expected to grow in the low single digits into the future.

A punishing standard

Regardless of where we are in the economic cycle, we know from history that sustaining long-term growth is just hard. Looking back over time, we see that the vast majority of companies in the Fortune 50 during the past several decades have stalled at one point or another. And when they do, they rarely fully recover and often don't ever restart growth at

1

all. Whether because of strategy, leadership, or external factors, the price paid has usually been high, as the majority of these companies lost more than 50 percent of their total market value when their stall occurred and they haven't yet gotten it back.

Sound like anything we know?

What boards and executive teams need are new ideas and new, untapped sources of growth. Wall Street is looking for those companies best positioned to capitalize on long-term growth trends. This means growth opportunities with certain characteristics: they'll be powered by sustainable and structural changes in the market; they'll be targeted on hot growth segments; they'll focus on products that tap into changing consumer behaviors and the largest, fastest growing geographies; and the risks associated with commercialization will be manageable.

Just get me to "The Number"

At the Latinum Network, we work alongside over 75 of the leading companies in the country, all of whom are actively targeting—and succeeding in—the U.S. Hispanic market. The theme we hear more than any other is the need for a consumer segment to be seen as central, and visibly contributing to, the company's overall strategy and business performance. If the Hispanic initiatives are indispensable to "getting to the corporate number," we win. If we're an add-on or "nice to have," we struggle to survive in turbulent times such as these.

Our on-again, off-again reality

That struggle often arises due to a disconnect between the opportunity associated with the U.S. Hispanic market on the one hand, and the vicious cycle of internal challenges on the other. It goes like this. By now, most companies have succeeded in communicating that this is an attractive opportunity to go after, but execution challenges often lead to unclear ROI, which in turns causes spotty commitment and an on-again, off-again approach to the market. And beyond that, internal champions are typically faced with skepticism about incremental spending. Justifying incremental spending for "just 17 percent of the U.S. population," answering questions about General Market backlash, and dealing with reflex responses like "Won't we just get them anyway?" typically distract organizations from paying the right level of attention to the U.S. Hispanic market.

Looking through the lens of Wall Street and the board

Our objective here is to share insights from the leading companies operating in the segment, with a specific focus on how Wall Street and the C-Suite evaluate and ultimately view the U.S. Hispanic market as an investment opportunity. We'll look at how investment cases are being made, the specific investment themes industry leaders are using to move resources and place bets, and a handful of strategies that capitalize on the opportunities and mitigate the risks identified by the investment community and senior executive team. So let's dive in.

A Great Growth Story to Tell

It's probably obvious at the start where we're going with this. In an era where market conditions make sustainable long-term growth opportunities exceedingly rare, the U.S. Hispanic segment stands out as a major exception. This, as we all know, is a story of growth. But even more interesting is the type of growth we're talking about. As we'll see, there are important characteristics of the opportunity that make this market even more attractive in the eyes of investors than is generally understood.

A uniquely American (that is, **domestic**) growth story

First of all, and this is obvious but sometimes underplayed, we're talking about a *domestic* investment opportunity. The U.S. Hispanic segment is an emerging market (by far the largest one) in a mature U.S. economy. Companies looking for growth on this kind of scale otherwise need to turn to international opportunities—the so-called BRIC countries (Brazil, Russia, India, China) or emerging markets overseas. While potentially attractive, these present a whole series of risks and uncertainties—political, macro-economic, currencies, culture, and so on—that companies don't have to deal with when investing at home.

Interested in new $100B markets?

And the scale associated with this market is huge. When we translate the headlines into the commercial opportunity, we see that over the past decade, U.S. Hispanic spending has increased as much as $100B every few years. This is analogous to the U.S. economy creating new markets of that size, and despite the recession (which we'll talk about more in a bit), we see this trend continuing consistently on into the future. With the non-Hispanic U.S. consumer economy projected to grow on average 0.4 percent per year over the next 40 years, there aren't too many other places we can look where spending is growing on such a large scale.

The engine: Population growth

Digging a little deeper, we see that most of the growth in spending (or purchasing power) that we're talking about is driven by population increases. We all know the numbers. The U.S. Hispanic population has been growing steadily the past four decades, and for the next 40 years will continue to grow, as much as 2 percent per year, about 3 to 4 times faster than the rest of the American population. And what's important is that this population growth accounts for a majority of the total growth in spending, with the balance coming from a range of other factors.

Not just growth, but the "good kind"

This matters, because growth powered by population changes is very different from growth that requires a bunch of assumptions around changes that may not materialize or be sustainable. Again, we already know a lot about these population dynamics: the U.S. Hispanic population will grow from 17 percent of the total to closer to 30 percent by 2050—but our focus here is on a deeper point. And that is, that population growth is a great way to power an investment opportunity. We know with close to certainty exactly how these population trends will play out over time—where the growth will come from, what this will mean for the population mix and household creation and other life stages, and all of the associated economic, educational, and generational changes. From the perspective of the investment opportunity, this type of growth is considered stable, predictable, and visible—all good things when it comes to placing value and risk judgments on investments.

The story is even more interesting than that

So population change is the key driver of this growth opportunity. However, there are four other important factors that help to paint the full picture. These include demographic changes, lifestyle trends, the economy, and the impact of acculturation. It's the interplay of all five of these factors that we need to understand to "get under the hood" of exactly what's driving spending, and we work with our member companies to apply the insights to investment decisions. What's good about this broader approach is that it puts culture in the proper context. Too often we see companies going straight to the question of whether there are true cultural differences that affect consumers' spending patterns. Sometimes there are, but it's even more true that spending is driven by other distinct differences as well, such as how much money the household makes, whether the adults are both working and seeking greater convenience, and the impact of the economy (both good and bad).

Ten years into a major market shift

We've done exhaustive analysis of the actual spending patterns and shifts of Hispanic consumers over the past 10 years, and see big changes that are relevant to understanding the investment opportunity. The biggest of these is the net increase of 15 million Hispanics, which we now know accounted for more than half the population growth of the country. Demographic shifts have also occurred, like the growth of native-born Hispanics, the youth segment boom, and even huge growth of older Hispanics. These have led to lifestyle and cultural shifts, as increased income and less time have made convenience more important, and the rise of native-born Hispanic millennials has had a widespread impact on acculturation.

And whole industries are shifting too

We also see these trends reflected in spending shifts. Over the ten years from 1999 to 2008, Hispanic spending growth was more than twice that of the rest of the economy in infants' and kids' products, education, health-care, and services for the elderly. Again, that's mostly powered by the population growth alone. The numbers change some when we convert them to spending growth per household, but the overall point remains the same. Hispanic household spending grew faster than the rest of the economy in all four of these industries. These are the kinds of data that investors look for as they evaluate investment opportunities in the segment.

Case-in-Point: Up the food convenience curve

We see these shifts playing out in a big way in the food, beverage, and restaurant (FB&R) sector. First of all, from a macro perspective, there was a 3-year period of time from 2005 to 2008 where Hispanic spending growth accounted for more than 100 percent of the growth of the U.S. FB&R sector. In other words, that $900+ billion industry would have completely stalled during that period if not for the growth in Hispanic spending. Going back to our 10-year look, the move up the convenience curve can be seen very clearly in the actual "wallet shift" away from scratch ingredients and canned foods and toward frozen and prepared foods and meals away from home. Even as this shifts plays out, though, another way to look at this—as investors do—is that Hispanic spending growth in all food categories was much higher than the rest of the population.

No refuge from the recession

Therefore, categories where Hispanics spend more money and where spending growth is highest are obvious candidates for investment consideration. And the 10-year numbers had painted a very clear picture. Unfortunately, we know that the recession has had a disproportionate impact on Hispanic households. At Latinum, we refer to the period from 2004 to 2007 as the "rising tide" for the Hispanic market—new households were being created, spending was growing, and (even beyond food) Hispanics represented the primary or only source of growth in many major categories. The recession has changed that picture. Hispanic incomes, jobs, and spending have been hard hit, and there's now a much more nuanced picture of Hispanics' contribution to category-level and overall economic performance.

Did You Know? Facts About the Hispanic Population

- While the U.S. Hispanic population is growing at over 3 percent a year, English-dominant Hispanics are growing even faster—at over 6 percent per year.

- There will be over 26 million "completely bicultural" U.S. Hispanics by the year 2020.

- The average Hispanic household has 3.8 people—compared to 2.6 in a non-Hispanic household.

- The fastest growing Hispanic DMAs with Hispanic populations over 50,000 are Memphis, New Orleans, and Columbus, Ohio.

Source: *American Community Survey 2006–2009*

But the longer-term trends will still play out

Investment strategies consider all time horizons, though, and we still see the same long-term trends playing out. While we don't know exactly how consumers (of all types) will respond in this economic recovery, there's still a lot to like about our story. The Hispanic population will likely grow by another 15 million people over the next 10 years; native-born Hispanics, youth, first-time households, and the aging will all significantly increase; lifestyle shifts will accompany wealth effects and contribute to some very interesting acculturation dynamics, including what we call "U-shaped curves" and retro-acculturation. New geographies are growing and new spending patterns being formed, all of which we've begun to forecast at Latinum to arm companies with the tools they need for 3-, 5-, and 10-year strategies and brand plans.

The heart of our investment case is long-term sustainable growth, powered by trends that are very stable and structural and will play out over a long period of time. Facts like where Hispanic households spend differently and how those spending patterns will be influenced and change going forward, help sharpen the case. But a domestic, population-driven investment opportunity of unequaled size is the heart of the story.

Investment Strategies for Navigating the New Market Realities

These are some of the ways Wall Street and executive teams look at the U.S. Hispanic investment opportunity relative to other growth bets they're evaluating. They are also elements of the full story that can be better told and more fully understood to ensure we're making the strongest possible case for the "next dollar" to be spent.

But this all only becomes real in practice when we get to the actual investment themes being used by Wall Street and the associated strategies being implemented by companies in the segment. We see many industry, and even category specific, analyses, but for our purposes here there are a number of broader themes and strategies in use. We work with our member companies building full strategies and plans for capturing the opportunity, and we provide an overview of the major ones here. In going through these, it'll become clear how they directly map back to the different ways CEOs think about getting to the corporate number.

Don't overlook what drives "the base"

A good first line to draw is between contribution to current performance and contribution to growth. The two are not mutually exclusive, but this is the delicate balancing act the corporation needs to pull off. And those things that drive today's performance—and provide the baseline from which future growth occurs—have a strong case to make for their share of resources to ensure ongoing success. In some companies, Hispanic consumers represent as much as 30 to 50 percent of current year sales. This is true nationally for some companies, and in multiple key markets or DMAs for many more. Comparing share of revenue generated or relative market share with the resources allocated to support these numbers is an effective investment theme in cases where a gap exists or more is needed to protect "the base."

Tap into the hottest segments (which are hot for different reasons)

Even as the overall Hispanic population grows, there are red-hot segments inside that companies should focus on. Native-born millennials have been growing at almost 5 percent per year, and by 2020 will add

4 million net new consumers to their ranks and represent 17 percent of the total Hispanic market. Add to this their influencer status at the center of their family and social networks, and they are a segment rightly commanding great attention. Growing even faster are aging Hispanics, at over 5 percent per year, with 6 million new consumers expected to be added here over the next 10 years. Other segments can be targeted for different reasons: moms as the key decision makers in the household and important consumers in their own right; youth, especially in certain markets; and men aged 21 to 49 since they have the most spending power of all these groups and also play a central role in the family.

Find the places where Hispanics drive growth

We talked about the food, beverage, and restaurant story before, but there's even more to it. Not only did the U.S. Hispanic segment represent over 100 percent of the growth in these industries from 2005 to 2008, but it also was the primary source of growth in over 60 percent of the more than 200 categories that make up this sector. The specifics are beyond our scope here, and they're fascinating to look at—a 10.2 percent spending growth CAGR in fish and seafood, 8.2 percent CAGR in candy and chewing gum, and so on, versus an actual decrease in spending coming from the rest of the U.S. economy. Even further, in the FB&R sector, there was another whole set of categories where Hispanic spending wasn't the only source of growth but was still the largest. This also holds true in other industries, such as personal care and household products. In situations like these, and there are a lot of them, this is obviously the lens to use when making the investment case for the segment relative to other available opportunities.

Or where they just spend more

There are three other ways to think about the "right" products to target based on Hispanic spending behaviors. First, Hispanic households spend more actual dollars on food (and scratch ingredients specifically) than non-Hispanics, despite lower income levels on average. Second, Hispanics spend a larger portion of their income on transportation, housing, apparel, food, and (therefore) retail. And third, Hispanics' spending levels are on the rise in areas such as education, entertainment, insurance, and pension products.

Tap fully into geographic movements

Sure, California, Texas, Florida, and New York. But Tennessee, Virginia, Georgia, and Iowa? With the release of new census data, it's clear that companies can no longer focus solely on traditional Hispanic areas. In fact, the highest growth areas are in cities in the South, Midwest, and Mid-Atlantic—places like Memphis, New Orleans, Columbus, and Baltimore. So now we see companies looking at a number of different ways to act on regional dynamics inside the Hispanic market—from states with the largest Hispanic populations, to states where the Hispanic population is most concentrated, to markets with the fastest Hispanic population growth. Even one level deeper than this is the composition of various regions by country of origin. It's no surprise that most regions are predominantly Mexican, but New England and the Mid-Atlantic are now a majority Caribbean, and the South Atlantic region is most diverse, with relatively even spreads across Mexican, Central American, and Caribbean Hispanics. In a world of limited resources where bets need to be placed, companies can target dollars on regional and local distribution and marketing strategies by following the emerging footprint of the Hispanic consumer.

Get to the "why" for category and brand development

The math here is well-understood. If Hispanic consumers or households under-index in certain categories or brands, then the value of closing that gap relative to non-Hispanics can be sized pretty readily. But that's just a numbers exercise. Where this gets real in practice is in the understanding of why spending differences might exist. We call this "demand driver analysis" and we can be very precise about exactly how much we'd expect a given consumer group to spend on a given category, based on the specific demographic and economic factors that determine demand and spending levels. Think about the presence or absence of children in the home driving spending for certain food products, asset ownership levels driving demand for financial services products, or income level or particular life stage driving demand for other categories. Cultural differences can also impact spending on a particular category (both up and down), but they need to be considered in the context of these (typically more meaningful) drivers of demand.

Close the General Market share gap

We recently conducted a major analysis for a leading CPG company of all its key brands and how they perform in the Hispanic segment relative to the rest of the market. They used this relative share difference as the "fair share" gap, and worked with us to understand the reasons for the gaps in share, to size the opportunity associated with closing (or decreasing) the gaps where possible, and the strategy and investment plan for doing so over the next 10 years. The result was a series of recommendations to produce incremental revenue lift of over $600M, without having to launch new products, enter new markets, or even activate new segments. There aren't too many places in the U.S. consumer economy today where such opportunities are available.

An aside: Be careful when using population as the benchmark

There are different forms of category and brand development that we've seen work—the share gap in Hispanic relative to the General Market, the share growth gap where the higher number serves as a high-water mark for what's possible in the market, and even the commonly used population benchmark that compares the percentage of total spend represented by Hispanics on a given category or brand and to the 17 percent population number. We see this talked about a lot, but prefer to use it for real investment cases only when adjusted up or down using the demand driver analysis just described.

Update investment themes for the realities of the recession

Companies are adjusting strategies in response to today's market realities. We've begun to develop a whole new map of consumer themes and associated strategies—things like volume packaging and budget versions of premium brands to reflect how Hispanic consumers now think about value, price, and loyalty; mobile and technology opportunities tapping into Hispanics' online behaviors; educational services which are hot across-the-board; and also themes such as health and wellness. And cutting across all of these, we see playing out in the market the emergence of a distinct U.S. Latino culture, which is becoming its own thing and producing opportunities related to fusion products, acknowledging their "innovator and influencer" status, and the maturity and pride that goes along with this cultural emergence.

Create new white space at the intersection of trends

Faced with the need to think differently, companies are getting creative and breaking compromises that have traditionally existed. Take the trade-off between convenience and authenticity. It's generally assumed that authentic tastes and flavors are more relevant when cooking with scratch ingredients. More convenient, ready-to-eat or ready-to-drink products don't have authentic flavors. We've seen some very interesting innovations that carve out new space with products that are both highly authentic as well as very convenient. One great example is Nestlé's launch of its Aguas Frescas drinks, which offer authentic flavors (Jamaica, Horchata, hibiscus, and tamarind) in a ready-to-drink package. Since launch, sales have exploded as the market reacts to this new innovation.

Or just decide the segment is a high-priority strategic growth bet

Then there's the relatively rare case where the executive team says it's not all about the numbers in the short-term. (In the long run, it's always at least in part about the numbers.) Here, the company makes a strategic commitment to win in the segment because it sees the value associated with being best positioned to capitalize on major, long-term trends. A great story for shareholder value creation over the long run attracts investment dollars. And having your shares and stock options be worth as much as possible upon retiring is something both the executive team and workforce can agree on.

Did You Know? Facts About Hispanic Consumption Growth Trends

- Between 1999 and 2008, Hispanics doubled their spending on restaurants—compared with around 45 percent growth for non-Hispanics; spending growth was even higher for education-related categories (207% vs. 68% for NH) and healthcare-related categories (117% vs. 37% for NH).

- Perhaps partially due to larger household sizes, Hispanics are more efficient buyers than non-Hispanics; on average, Hispanics spend only about 60 percent to 80 percent per person vs. non-Hispanics on most food categories.

- Hispanic aggregate spend growth per year is over 4% in many categories, comprising up to 50+ percent of total spend growth in many categories.

Source: *Consumer Expenditure Survey 1999–2008*

A Note on Risk and Complexity

From an investor's perspective, there are a number of risks associated with investing in opportunities focused on the U.S. Hispanic market. These include questions related to the timing of the trend being realized, how companies will get paid, the impact of inflation and commodity price increases, pricing power, private labeling, whether all of this is already reflected in the company's stock price, and how the market will actually trade on the trend. What's interesting is how closely the technical issues actually mirror strategy decisions, including the central marketing question of what's incremental to the Hispanic segment versus what is already captured in companies' total market strategies.

These risks are real, but all investment opportunities come with risk. The strategies here show the different dimensions of the Hispanic opportunity and the different lenses companies use to evaluate potential investments in the segment. There's no one-size-fits-all approach, but companies that understand and directly address the questions asked by the investment community and executive team have the best chance to win the battle for the next available dollar. We believe that investments like these, which leverage larger-scale trends and connect the dots in new and creative ways, will have a major impact on the commercial opportunity and corporate strategies.

A Final Word

It's time to return to growth. And while long-term growth opportunities are hard to come by, the U.S. Hispanic market stands out as a very attractive option. And this isn't just because we want it be so. The reality is, far beyond the overall size of the market that we all talk about, it's exactly the kind of investment opportunity companies are looking for. It's powered by sustainable and structural changes in the market; it targets a hot segment; it's focused on products that align well with changing consumer behaviors and the largest, fastest growing geographies; and the risks associated with commercialization are manageable. Companies that understand how the investment community evaluates and views the Hispanic opportunity, and allocate resources accordingly, will be best positioned to capitalize on the long-term trend.

This is a story unlike any other playing out in Corporate America. We own it and it's up to us to tell it effectively.

The Latinum Network is the premier business network that assists brands in taking advantage of the growing U.S. Hispanic market through strategic analytics, cutting-edge research and peer-to-peer collaboration. Latinum Network assists executives and their teams in developing deeper insights into the market, more effective strategies for the segment, and the solutions required to successfully design and execute core marketing initiatives. The company currently has over 70 members including some of the nation's most recognizable brands. Latinum Network is a wholly owned business of EcoNet Ventures LLC. *www.latinumnetwork.com*

Why Hispanics in the Boardroom Today?

Carlos F. Orta
President and CEO, Hispanic Association on Corporate Responsibility (HACR)

ACCORDING to the 2010 Census, the Hispanic community in the United States exceeded 50 million consumers, not including 3.7 million Puerto Rican Islanders. Every month, 50,000 Hispanics turn 18 years of age. There are more Hispanics in the United States than there are Canadians in Canada. Hispanics make up the largest number of minority college students in the United States. Our collective buying power surpassed $1 trillion in 2010 and it is growing at $75 to $100 billion per year. By 2015, it is projected to reach $1.5 trillion. In addition, Hispanics will constitute about 30 percent of the total population of the United States by 2050.

Yet, in spite of these gains, in 2011 Hispanics are under-represented in almost every sector of our society—in government, nonprofits, and at Fortune 500 companies. As of this writing, there are only seven male Hispanic chief executive officers in the Fortune 500, and we know of only one Latina CEO in the Fortune 1000.

Hispanic Association on Corporate Responsibility (HACR) is a non-partisan, not-for-profit advocacy organization representing 16 national Hispanic organizations in the United States and Puerto Rico. As president and chief executive officer of HACR, I am proud that Hispanic inclusion on corporate boards is one of four corporate social responsibility and market reciprocity pillars, with the others being employment, procurement, and philanthropy.

In 2004, HACR, along with Catalyst, the Executive Leadership Council (ELC), and the executive search firm Prout Group, partnered and created the Alliance for Board Diversity (ABD). In 2008, the Leadership Education for Asian Pacifics (LEAP) joined ABD, and this past May at the HACR Symposium, ABD released our third census report. The report found that:

- Fortune 500 boards were less diverse than Fortune 100 boards.

- Men held close to 85 percent of all board seats. White men dominated the boardroom, holding 77.6 percent of board seats. Minority men held 6.8

15

percent. White women held 12.7 percent. Minority women held 3 percent.

- More specifically, African-American women held 1.9 percent of Fortune 500 board seats; Hispanic women held 0.7 percent; Asian Pacific Islander women held 0.3 percent; African-American men held 2.7 percent; Hispanic men held 2.3 percent; and Asian Pacific Islander men held 1.8 percent.

- Women and minorities were significantly underrepresented in Fortune 500 board leadership positions. White men held 94.9 percent of board chair positions.

- There was not a single Latina lead director or board chair.

Speaking of Hispanic inclusion, friend and mentor, George Herrera, (board member of Wyndham Worldwide) says it best, "If we are good enough to market to and buy your products, then we should be good enough to be included in senior management and on corporate boards."

So what action is HACR and the Hispanic community taking to highlight the issue of under-representation and to begin to change the playing field?

HACR recently launched a two-year campaign called "Advocate," which highlights the issues of under-representation through print ads, via Twitter, and by the release of HACR's first documentary film, *Insider Game,* which tells an intriguing and compelling story of commitment to our community from corporate leaders who understand that in order to move the needle forward and be successful, you have to play an insider game.

As always, HACR will continue to advocate for change in how corporations think about, measure, engage with, and interact around Hispanic inclusion at the workplace, in the boardroom, and within the community.

Corporate America benefits and shareholder value increases from the insights and expertise that Hispanic board members contribute to the new marketplace reality. Long-term growth and sustainability is a corporate imperative that only the Hispanic market can deliver in the U.S. today.

Hispanic Association on Corporate Responsibility (HACR) is one of the most influential advocacy organizations in the nation representing 16 national Hispanic organizations in the United States and Puerto Rico. Our mission is to advance the inclusion of Hispanics in Corporate America at a level commensurate with our economic contributions. To that end, HACR focuses on four areas of corporate responsibility and community reciprocity: employment, procurement, philanthropy, and governance. *www.hacr.org*

Diversity as an Engine of Innovation

Alison Kenney Paul
Vice chairman and U.S. Retail & Distribution Leader, Deloitte, LLP

INCREASINGLY, retailers and consumer goods companies must embrace diversity as a market force, and that includes diversifying their workforces—not simply to do what is right, but because a diverse employee base will drive affinity with and understanding of the customer.

Forging those connections effectively and for the long term depends, to a significant degree, on having an employee population that reflects the population overall, as well as specific communities served.

Appealing to a carefully segmented, diverse market is no longer only a niche opportunity for adventurous store managers and edgy entrepreneurs: multiculturalism is fast becoming a retail and consumer goods industry opportunity too big to ignore.

Purchasing dollars among Whites increased by 139 percent between 1990 and 2008; growth in the same timeframe was 187 percent among African Americans, 349 percent among Hispanics, 337 percent among Asians, and 213 percent among Native Americans. In particular, the Hispanic market increasingly represents a larger proportion of all buyers as it is expanding in size more rapidly than other groups.

The good news for employers is that diverse employees comprise a growing part of the overall talent pool. Growth of the U.S. labor market between 2010 and 2018 is being projected at about 6 percent, with increases among diverse workers the primary drivers of that expansion. For example, Hispanic workers are expected to increase in that timeframe by 27 percent, followed by Asians at 23 percent, then African Americans at 9 percent, and Whites at 4 percent.

Retailers and consumer goods companies that recruit their share of these new entrants at all levels of the organization may realize the opportunity represented by an enhanced cultural mix. This may include added perspective on marketing and merchandising campaigns; improved strategic decision-making; and the benefits of these workers' direct interactions with customers on the selling floors.

Ultimately strong recruiting, retention, and development initiatives can build sustainability of the multicultural talent pool and become a self-perpetuating cycle of investing in and receiving value.

Top management should view workforce diversity not as a standalone program but as an essential element of their organization's value proposition and a critical ingredient of their business survival. Moreover, they should demonstrate openness to fresh ideas and ensure that mere tolerance for differences is replaced by a commitment to inclusion. Rather than lip service, they should actively and genuinely embrace that which makes people different—even unique—in their experiences and aspirations as well as their physical and cultural distinctions.

By these actions, company leaders can lay the foundation for better insights about their customers, improved loyalty from diverse consumers who see themselves in the employees by whom they're served, and enhanced results from both employee recruiting and new business development efforts. Retail organizations and consumer goods companies focused in a meaningful and credible way on diversity can inspire purchases and loyalty with entire populations of consumers who experience the regard, respect, and affinity they seek.

chapter 2

The Chief Marketing Officer Perspective

S-M-A-R-T Growth through Opportunity Right-Sizing

Carlos Santiago
Chief Strategist, Santiago Solutions Group

ONE of the biggest obstacles in growing Hispanic market share is accurately sizing the prize of the market opportunity for products and services. Over a decade of strategy consulting among hundreds of clients and tens of categories, we have found that business managers are hungry for making solid, well informed "go or no-go" decisions, setting objectives that the organization can realistically undertake, and determining where and how much to invest for optimal growth and reasonable ROI. Investment decisions commensurate to the right size of the business opportunity avoid myopic initiatives plagued with what I call the "dimmer syndrome": *on today, cut to the bones in six months, shut off in two years, on-again when the stock is high and killed again when key Hispanic talent leaves the organization.* In my experience, Hispanic opportunity right-sizing allows companies to keep the switch "on" because it leads to **S-M-A-R-T** business growth; namely, growth that is Sustainable, Methodical, Aligned, Responsible and Timely.

> **Sustainable** Growth requires consistency, which can only be delivered by investment and resource allocation commensurate to the opportunity.

> **Methodical** The methodology used to assess that opportunity must be true and tested, based on scientific approaches tailored to the realities of the particular business and the categories it competes in.

Aligned Corporate wide organizational alignment and the corresponding accountability across functional areas and business units are the glue that keeps it together. Without alignment, new strategies and tactics may be at odds with existing plans, leaving little chance to capture the opportunity and deliver results.

Responsible A rush to growth for growth's sake, without a profit or ROI goal, leads to inefficient allocation of resources, negatively impacting results and hence, the company's bottom line.

Timely Timing the opportunity is just as important as the opportunity itself. The organization must be able to deliver the brand's promise at the same rate or faster than the incremental opportunity it is pursuing over and above business as usual.

Effective Growth Leaders

Effective Growth Leaders are methodical about right-sizing the Hispanic—and all business opportunities—across their portfolios. They know that a solid, fact-based approach is necessary for identifying and aligning interdependent functions, garnering buy-in, integration, and support across silos, and of course, securing resources, ultimately rallying the company behind a common growth objective that everyone can recite from the board room to the frontlines.

Conversely, some Hispanic marketers take dangerous shortcuts relying on unreliable data sources, half-baked input, gut-feel or "guesstimates," simplistic approaches, and faulty models that yield unrealistic expectations. The organization is left with disappointing results and no pragmatic approach to recalibrate, optimize, and drive long-term growth. Worst of all, these shortcuts can end up creating a perception that Latino initiatives simply do not deliver sustainable growth and ROI.

To make Hispanic efforts succeed, organizations must assign proper resources beyond marketing and communications including capital, people with a mature, hands-on skill set, and guidance in Hispanic business and marketing at all levels; IT, infrastructure, focused incentives, customer experience enhancements, product development, research, and continuous learning platforms among others. In our experience, the biggest risk to Hispanic business growth does not come from competitors. Instead, sustainable growth is thwarted in great part by lack of strategic alignment, lack of Hispanic marketing expertise among middle-managers, and poorly made investment decisions.

In sum, right-sizing the Hispanic market opportunity is the foundation for S-M-A-R-T business growth.

It incorporates a cohesive body of the right analytics and reliable data inputs, the right internal and external assessments, the right multicultural business know-how and acumen, the right insights, and the right forward-looking analytics. It leads to growth objectives over and above business as usual that are challenging yet attainable through sound strategies, tactics, and investment decisions. So let's talk about what happens when the opportunity sizing is not quite *right*.

Five Common Pitfalls in Sizing the Market Opportunity

1. "Super-sizing" the opportunity

The most common mistake is "super-sizing" the Hispanic business opportunity. Back of the envelope approaches like only using BDI data (Brand Development Index), CDI data (Category Development Index) and "fair-share" estimates, magically claim the growth potential as an extrapolation of high-performing markets (i.e., geographies or Hispanic sub-segments) on top of lower performing ones. Regardless of the business category being targeted, claiming *"the whole Hispanic market as a growth opportunity"* is unrealistic; it has to be evaluated on a one-on-one basis.

While some markets may share many similarities, no two geographic markets or Hispanic consumer sub-segments are exactly alike. Consumers bond with brands for different reasons and at different levels, depending, for example, on the degree of brand heritage (known or unknown brand or category in country of origin) which means that brand consideration funnels can vary significantly across markets. From brand saliency to consumer conversion, to usage levels and brand loyalty, Hispanic sub-segments and geographies often reveal different levels of purchase behaviors that dictate diverse levels of potential growth. In other words, one blanket performance goal does not fit all.

As any marketer knows, consumer traits vary in the U.S. from North to South and East to West. Similarly, Latino immigrants from different regions in their country of origin, say amid Mexico's Norteños (immigrants from Tamaulipas, Nuevo Leon, Coahuila, and Chihuahua in the north of Mexico) and Capitalinos (immigrants from the Distrito Federal), also bring different and varying degrees of brand loyalties that affect U.S. brand choices in distinctive ways. For example, Norteños tend to settle in the Southwestern region of the U.S., predominantly Texas markets. Tecate beer enjoys its strongest market share, distribution and recognition among Norteños, so it will also enjoy a natural advantage among immigrants in Texas. That natural advantage disappears on the East coast since Tecate is not available in the Caribbean or South America.

Macro and microeconomic conditions as well as each Hispanic market's unique composition of socio-economics, occupations, generational mix, acculturation levels, and language preferences exercise a given muscle on potential growth.

In planning a winning strategy, a visiting team would not disregard the home advantage or specific strengths of an opposing baseball team. Their average batting record and playing tactics are similar to historical sales trends and strategies. Therefore, the easiest way to over-promise opportunity is to apply blanket ratios and generalize attainable market shares and growth rates with disregard for the specific market conditions. Fully understanding Hispanic geographic and psychographic nuances is critically important to estimating realistic market opportunities.

Finally, just as you must have introspection for a true sense of your aptitudes in order to succeed, a pragmatic internal assessment of the corporate strengths and weaknesses will uncover levers and hurdles that may enable or hinder the organizational ability to attain discrete growth levels. For example, disregarding distribution levels, let alone your brands' ability to compete in elusive channels (i.e., c-stores, independents, bodegas, or online) or your ability to compete against direct marketers (i.e., multilevel, catalogs and DRTV), could force major set backs in your market growth plans. Furthermore, messaging and ad spend could be muted by what we call "distribution mismatch;" weak distribution or lack of stores located within proximity to the ideal Hispanic sub-target.

How right-sizing works

To provide perspective, let's look at an opportunity sizing case study for a retail client. An initial assessment showed that the largest business potential was in the Los Angeles market, not surprisingly since it is by far the largest Hispanic market in the United States. However, as we delved into the opportunity and assessed the areas near the retailer's stores, it became evident that few were located in *Spanish-dominant, non-acculturated* Latino areas, making that sub-segment of the Hispanic market opportunity null and void. Thus, we zeroed out that opportunity in the short-term.

However, the alignment of the opportunity among *Bilingual-Bicultural* (i.e., more acculturated) Latinos with the client store saturation in the areas in which they tend to reside and work turned out to be a perfect match. Consequently, we did not recommend tackling the entire Los Angeles Hispanic market opportunity pronto but rather focused on the *Bilingual-Bicultural* portion of the opportunity in the short-term, creating the retail client's "point of entry" strategy targeting only the Bilingual segment. The client was left with an aggressive, yet realistic strategy to act upon and measure immediately while addressing the longer term opportunities for expansion. It was music to their ears!

2. Malnourishing the opportunity

Just as dangerous as "super-sizing" an opportunity is malnourishing the growth potential. Low-balling may not only kill the Hispanic opportunity all together, but also it shortchanges the needed momentum to significantly impact your target consumers across touch-points to drive their mindset and preference for your products or services. Malnourishing the growth potential is a common trap of opportunity sizing efforts, and demonstrates a lack of understanding of the new marketplace. It comes about as a result of perceived scant growth potential that does not reach the scale needed to invest adequately and transform consumer behavior while attaining a reasonable ROI. Malnourished Hispanic growth initiatives do not produce the intended market impact, nor do they generate the traction needed to become an integral part of an organization's recognized growth drivers. They will not survive. Think about a crop with insufficient water, fertilizer, and the appropriate balance of sun and shade. Are those the best conditions to reap a record-breaking harvest? For similar reasons, poor Hispanic market data and poor sizing practices that yield artificially conservative estimates are unable to secure sufficient resources and end up choking the real growth potential.

3. Piggy-backing on shallow assumptions

Opportunity right-sizing depends on a carefully selected set of assumptions. A frequent mistake in sizing opportunities is to confine the potential to the existing user profile and its current product or service use patterns. Relying on strategies that reach exactly the same customer as you have today will greatly limit your brands' growth potential. Such a strategy is just a projection of business as usual, not an assessment of real Hispanic business growth potential. While there is comfort in the tried and proven, competitors that cannot innovate and grow out of a shallow consumer base and diminishing average expenditure, eventually do become extinct.

For example, a direct marketer that went after the same consumer profile year after year was quite successful at optimizing repeat purchases and even average items per order and total dollars per customer. Yet, the marketer became frustrated at single-digit growth from its narrow but deep Hispanic base. A thorough opportunity analysis identified that the biggest prize was in persuading a whole new customer base that was not fully satisfied by its competitors. Sizing this new base, understanding its needs and triggers to purchase, uncovered enough opportunity to leap to a new growth curve. Eventually, the client accelerated its trends to double-digit growth rates. The brand was fortified and its growth achieved stronger sustainability by successfully widening its franchise.

Growing segments to their full potential takes into account the development of new or at least enhanced products, customer experience, and go-to-market strategies to meet unmet as well as often unspoken consumer needs. Conventional assessments such as quantitative research methods and traditional focus groups may miss verbal and non-verbal cues, emotions and behaviors that may lead to breakthrough insights for innovation. Using systematic consumer research approaches such as listening to consumers in different environments, carefully observing their behaviors, as well as the behavior of different channels of distribution, and front-line employees, will provide direction and context for strategy development and implementation that is not obvious or readily available.

Finally, be wary of low-balling your assumptions based on previous poor outcomes. Just because the business tried reaching out to the Hispanic market in the past, whether through a pilot or large-scale Hispanic effort that did not deliver on the expected ROI, it does not mean that there is no growth from this market segment. It may well be the result of poor planning, lack of adequate resource allocation across the organization, or ineffective execution. Saying, "We tried it once and it did not work so let's not invest as much this year," is not a fact-based approach to size the opportunity. Unless you dissect the many components that went into it, including your real opportunity and corresponding resources, the rearview mirror should not dictate your future opportunity.

4. Employing "dirty" data

Another common pitfall that costs companies millions every year is using data of uneven quality without proper adjustment factors. Hispanic information and intelligence has improved by leaps and bounds and continues to get better, more accessible, and economical. However, many internal company databases, intelligence systems, and widely available syndicated studies come with "blind spots" that may under-represent the size of the prize by huge factors. Some syndicated studies leave out sampling many Hispanic markets, Hispanic sub-segments, or certain "classes" of stores like independents, mom and pop bodegas, swap meets, "boticas," convenience stores, gas station stores, liquor stores, and even giant discounters like Walmart. Think about where you buy products "on-the-go" like candies, snacks, breath mints, bottled water, spirits, sport drinks, and so on. If you based your sizing purely on one of these syndicated studies you could miss out on sizing and getting funding for 15 to 40 percent of the opportunity.

Let me share the example of a new snack brand we helped out a few years ago and pardon if I'm somewhat spotty in order to maintain anonymity. The top down approach that guided them to size the Hispanic opportunity prior to our engagement was based on the same syndicated data source that they subscribed to corporately, but they applied it to the Hispanic market at face value. Unfortunately, this is a common mistake among Hispanic marketers, even among companies that have been involved in Hispanic marketing for years.

First, the Hispanic data was based on only four markets. Second, the data reflected purchase patterns only from large chains with more than $2 million in sales. It excluded high-density Hispanic neighborhoods retailers—some small and some quite large independent chains—where Latino urban dwellers buy daily staples like milk, diapers, and beer. The estimate did not account for Walmart or the "contraband" volume from its own company's SKUs crossing the Mexican border into U.S. markets. Our research tracked this "contraband" as far North as San Jose, even Oregon and Washington. In aggregate, these factors represented an underestimation of 62 percent of the real Hispanic volume even before overlaying growth prospects. The brand's Hispanic annual profit margin, from which marketing investment was decided, proved to be undersized by $30.5 million. And, all that contribution had been assumed to be generated by the "general" (non-Hispanic) market. The same syndicated data was "scrubbed," combined with internal corporate data and primary research to make "safe" adjustments and fill the gaps.

Performing advanced analytics on top of "dirty" fundamentals not only minimizes the opportunity, but it also often results in a waste of limited resources with regretful results and negative returns. Powerful consumer databases can deliver sizable growth prospects and are useful as long as they accurately capture not only brand level usage data, but also Hispanic demographics, acculturation, language preferences, and behavior. We've often seen corporate clients use incomplete data sources. We've also seen clients repeatedly relying on databases containing high incidences of bad addresses and incomplete household purchase behaviors that were projected from few Latino respondents at the category level. Left uncounted, these deficiencies lead to inaccurate marketing, and retail strategies, or targeting of household addresses, emails, or phone numbers that ruin your ability to bring in the expected ROI results even if the advertising messages and everything else is on strategy.

I am sure you have received recurring electronic offers for products or services that don't get close to your needs. Not only does this minimize a campaign's effectiveness, but also it may lead to backlash as consumers grow to resent the marketer or the brand and stop trusting the sender.

Let me be more precise. If you are using Hispanic databases fueled by government statistics like the Consumer Expenditure Survey (CES) published by the U.S. Department of Labor Statistics, keep in mind that the Hispanic sample of many counties in this survey may be too small to project accurately to the entire county (for example, ten or fewer Latinos participated in the survey). Applying data across all the Hispanic households, zip codes, or census tracts in the county as "imputed" data from these few Hispanic participants, can yield abysmal and wrong results. Furthermore, as previously mentioned, such purchase data does not apply equally to all brands in a category and must be adjusted accordingly.

Finally, "dirty" data exists across sources and research methodologies. For example, there is little to gain from Hispanic research based on English-only interviews or insufficient Spanish language samples, unless you plan to grow your business only from English-dominant Hispanics. All inputs must therefore be analyzed in detail to ensure the opportunity assessment is truly right-sized to you.

5. Banking on inoperable growth

A growth opportunity model is numbers driven. In other words, it uses actual figures (i.e., historical sales) and percentages (i.e., growth rates) to arrive at a new set of growth targets. But these targets are devoid of operational intelligence. Specifically, they do not account for the time, effort, segment marketing expertise, and readiness required to implement a growth plan that captures incremental opportunity. Incremental growth more often than not requires innovative thinking and analytical approaches. That means doing some things differently from the way they have been done in the past. While it requires challenging the organization to stretch its goals, it must be operationally feasible to achieve. Synchronizing and orchestrating the capabilities of internal functions and their go-to-market tactics is akin to infusing the numbers with a reality check that impacts growth rates and scaling, thus, calibrating the sizing model across time and Hispanic marketing and sales expertise.

Remember the retailer case study we discussed earlier? In order to capture growth opportunities within the less-acculturated, Spanish-dominant Hispanics, the retailer needed to open new stores. While it was already very adept at doing so, it needed to build higher levels of cultural competence into its operations. This kind of expansion had implications that spanned from product design, to logistics to human resources, to mention only a few.

There is no such thing as placing brands—or businesses—on steroids and taking a step back to marvel at their miracle growth. Each interdependent business function plays a role on the successful delivery of the growth. Managers of those functions need to be inspired and motivated to move in sync with careful planning to close gaps and gain new skill sets. For example, the sales organization might need to become more culturally competent, gain product distribution in new channels and develop strategic *In-Culture* channel partnerships. Product marketing might need time to adjust to a segment marketing matrix organization. Marketing communications might be slow to uncover culturally relevant strategic insights, and become adept at turning these insights into effective in-language messaging. The multicultural staff might be able to pursue only a modest growth rate in the short term by seizing the low hanging fruit while attaining new knowledge that can be applied towards more challenging conversions of higher-value prospects. All these interlocking pieces need to buy into the incremental growth potential, needing motivation and support to stay focused despite competing priorities.

There's another important factor to consider regarding operationalizing growth plans that is best explained by the crop analogy used earlier. What happens to soil that has been hard hit by severe drought and improper maintenance? Not only does it deliver a substandard harvest, but also, if left unattended, it's overall quality will be diminished. It will therefore require additional resources to reinstate it to its productive potential. Likewise, unsuccessful past Hispanic efforts require first an awareness that this may be the case, and secondly deliberate tactics and resources to overcome negatively biased internal (functional areas) and external (customers and consumers) conditions. Also, past experiences may have left the organization with a high degree of skepticism about the attractiveness and suitability of the Hispanic market. Right-sizing goes only so far without proper internal communications, buy-in, and training on cultural know-how that raises the level of comfort that the organization can be successful in a new approach and thereby ensures commitment.

Your customers are very likely to have also suffered. They may have been left with a bitter taste in their mouths from a less-than-acceptable customer experience or simply have no emotional brand relationship. It is therefore important to incorporate the timing and resources required to rebuild credibility and trust. A low quality of customer experience can wipe out your opportunity for growth before you become aware of the problem. It is important to track satisfaction levels regarding customer experience and the readiness and frequency of recommending the brand to a friend or family member along with other metrics.

A research study completed by Santiago Solutions Group among service categories including financial, health care and insurance, and subscription TV, indicated that high quality customer service in Spanish is a pivotal differentiating factor when Hispanics make purchasing decisions and decide to continue doing business with companies. In fact, 9 in 10 respondents said they would consider doing more business as a result of an excellent customer service experience, 4 in 10 respondents who received excellent customer service indicated they would "tell friends and family," and 3 out 4 said they would consider canceling their service and telling others if they had an unsatisfactory customer service experience.

It's Not Rocket Science

Growth, by definition, is dynamic. It requires looking at the business from fresh vantage points. All too often marketers are so immersed in their day-to-day that they do not interact with target consumers in the real-life situations which they purchase and use their brands, categories and or substitutes. This is why many **Effective Growth Leaders** have come to rely increasingly more on external experts that apply advanced analytics as well as understand the market dynamics, validating assumptions, testing hypotheses for leaping into new growth curves, incorporating the right kind of intelligence and ultimately right-sizing the Hispanic opportunity. They know that right-sizing the Hispanic market is more than a potential opportunity, but rather a key to their business' long term health and S-M-A-R-T business growth.

7 Habits of Effective Growth Leaders

Effective Growth Leaders —

- Use a dual approach to opportunity right-sizing. First, a top-down approach that use syndicated research and internal analytics to identify the big trees in the forest, a category and product portfolio opportunity mapping. Then, they follow with a grounds-up volumetric approach with primary research to add consumer dimensions and fresh insights while increasing the overall reliability of the opportunity model.

- Develop front-to-back-end strategies that innovate sales processes, fix infrastructure gaps, and uncover new insights that trigger new brand trial, increase relevance, engage old and new consumers more regularly and create tight communities of fans that become voluntary active brand ambassadors.

- Pursue new sub-segments, continuously develop new products, new customer relationships, new value propositions and business models to reenergize their growth curves. They are masters at innovation that effectively expand their franchises faster than their competitors.

- Develop focused but not isolated Hispanic strategies. There needs to be symmetry between the Hispanic and the overall corporate growth strategy. Identifying and tapping into existing synergies will result in faster and higher ROI.

- Understand that Hispanic market growth typically entails some similar and some different approaches than non-Hispanic market growth models. Many categories reflect less developed Hispanic consumer segments, thus, they have the patience, foresight and discipline to recalibrate, make adjustments and keep a long-term outlook.

- Pay vital attention to creating key success factors and tracking growth diagnostics that appear in shared scorecards across the organization. The full size of the prize is attainable if incentives are tied to results and there is broad ownership of the growth goal beyond the multicultural unit.

- Tailor their growth opportunity sizings to the internal holder of the funds. Increasingly, the boss is not the CMO but rather the CFO. Don't underestimate their involvement and applying sound financial methods to your opportunity modeling.

Santiago Solutions Group (SSG) is a thought leader in strategy and management consulting, creating innovative multicultural business strategies. SSG's strategic framework focuses on quantifying the core target segments' upside revenue potential vis-à-vis its acculturation trigger points through an array of proprietary methodologies. The company's 5-Ps strategic blueprints empower corporate planning and marketing teams, as well as ad agencies, to conceive multicultural programs capable of sustaining traction. *www.santiagosolutionsgroup.com*

Challenges for Agencies, Marketers, and CEOs

Jessica Pantanini

COO of Bromley Communications and
Former President, Association of Hispanic Advertising Agencies (AHAA)

Vision

Most CEOs and boards can see the opportunity that the diverse American community means for their business, and often direct their teams to focus on multicultural as a strategic imperative. Unfortunately, several challenges exist for Corporate America from vision to execution.

Wall Street likes short-term thinking

The emphasis on short-term results driven by Wall Street, has had an impact in the marketing space:

- Marketers are not focused on long-term relationships with consumers or agency partners, but rather, the quickest way to impress the higher-ups in order to get promoted or meet goals for bonuses. They end up looking for quick, splashy ideas that have potential impact in the short term, but are not necessarily effective for the long term.

- Marketers have too much on their plates. The last thing they want to think about is the ethnic space. Often it's unfamiliar territory, and therefore they think it best to focus their efforts where they are comfortable and are secure in being able to deliver results.

- Resources are tight. Having to spread their dollars across a variety of segments causes marketers to find the easy solution, not the best one. For years, Corporate America has been trying to find the easy way to handle this increasingly complicated market, from media divergence, to multicultural growth. They have yet to find it.

- When they actually do invest, marketing strategies get whittled down to the same old formulaic traditional media approach (i.e., traditional broadcast media), not the most effective way to reach consumers in this increasingly diverse media marketplace.

Talent

The best and brightest are not usually tapped for leading the charge within Corporate America. Corporate managers struggle with diversity and typically tap people because they come from the relevant market segment, not necessarily because they have passion for it. To make matters worse, being in a multicultural position pigeonholes professionals, stagnating their professional growth because these positions often are seen as less than a line brand management position.

Clients tasked with the responsibility of leading the charge often do not have the support of middle management. They are constantly selling and re-selling the opportunity within their own organizations. This situation is exacerbated by the fact that CMOs' tenure is on average a mere 18 to 24 months.

General Market

When talking about the General Market, theory and practice are often at odds. We tend to refer to the General Market as anything that is not ethnic. Yet, in practice, when communication goals are set, they are against the total population. Marketers do separate research, tracking studies, and more often than not, briefs are written without the inclusion of ethnic insights. How can a brief be written for a General Market population, which targets all people regardless of ethnicity, without the inclusion of ethnic insights in today's diverse population?

The biggest mistake clients make today is putting the General Market agency in charge, and not taking charge themselves. Too few clients at the CMO level have relationships with their ethnic agencies. Including ethnic partners and giving them a seat at the table is the best way to ensure that work will be inclusive.

The leadership of the General Market agencies, like that of Corporate America, sees the opportunity, but because they lack diversity at their highest levels they don't understand the changes they need to make in order for the vision to become a reality. They lack perspective.

In a recent meeting with a well-known Senator, we discussed the need for women to get more involved in politics and how the unique perspective of women changes the dialogue. For example, defense: When discussing that subject, men tend to focus on the number of assets the military has, whereas women ask questions about PTSD or the divorce rate among military families. This diversity in participation broadens the conversation.

In order for marketing to be most effective, the process must be more inclusive. If you want to win for the long term, you must ensure that all your partners have a seat at the table from beginning to end. If you want it done right, do it yourself. Don't delegate the responsibility to your General Market agency.

Recommendations

Reward marketing managers for properly managing the holistic portfolio of your brand via the development and execution of long-term strategic multicultural initiatives:

- Stay involved in multicultural.

- Create performance evaluation metrics that are tied to multicultural efforts and their success.

- Develop a career path for multicultural division leaders and teams to ensure that they are integrated into the overall marketing team, and have a clear opportunity for continued growth.

- Get to know your ethnic agencies (especially important for CMOs and CEOs)

- Secure up-and-coming talent by conducting job fairs with key organizations like National Society of Hispanic MBAs.

- If holistic work is your goal, ensure that your ethnic agencies are involved with leading strategic development as an equal partner with General Market agencies.

All of us at **Bromley Communications** call ourselves originators—believers in the power of ideas to originate change in consumer's behavior and grow brands. We start with an ownable consumer truth. Armed with an understanding of consumer needs, desires and values, we create communications that speak to them in a truthful and respectful way, never forcing a preconceived brand message, but empowering the consumer to form their own connection. We believe that the stronger the connection between consumer and brand, the more powerfully we can originate change in the market. *www.bromley.biz*

Retailing for Success — In-Culture

Marie Quintana
Sr. Vice President, Multicultural Marketing and Sales, PepsiCo

Don't overlook any part of the retail universe

It is not rocket science but common sense. The best marketing and strategic planning and the most up-to-date insights and know-how will miss the greatest opportunity for ROI if the products that consumers need and want are not "at arm's length" where they go to shop and when they need them and want them. It is that simple.

As established earlier in this book, the U.S. Hispanic population represents a very attractive and proven growth opportunity for both consumer goods companies and retailers. However, it is critically important for all parties involved to understand why shoppers select specific retail channels. When targeting Hispanic consumers, the retail universe needs to be re-thought and its horizon widened. Why? Because the Hispanic retail universe includes a much wider range of non-traditional, independent stores than the General Market retail universe. A typical Hispanic family shopping week can include visits to bodegas, convenience stores, *panaderias* (bakeries), dollar stores, and *carnicerias* (meat stores) as well as General Market grocery stores (both national and regional retail chains), Hispanic grocery stores, drug stores, superstores, and warehouse clubs. And that's true regardless of Hispanic consumer levels of acculturation.

How manufacturers can win with Hispanics

It is important, first, to be aware of the numerous retail options available to the Latino shopper and, second, to know how to use these different channels to speak to Hispanics in ways that are relevant to them. Next, you need to develop successful retail programs and to ensure the right strategy for great results. Several components need to be considered and executed for success:

1. Develop a great relationship with retailers,

2. Obtain culturally relevant shopper insights,

3. Identify the right brand and product assortment to appeal to different Latino families. The Hispanic market is not monolithic; there is much cultural variation in brand and product assortment preferences depending on country of origin and degree of acculturation.

4. Create relevant and engaging shopper marketing programs that appeal to the entire family,

5. Get close to the Hispanic community to create emotional connections and develop long-term brand loyalty.

I will address these in greater detail later in the chapter.

What drives store selection?

Understanding what triggers an Hispanic shopper to turn to a particular store or channel requires retailers and their product suppliers to understand the basics:

The Latino family and its shopping dynamics. For example, who in the family does the actual shopping versus who is being shopped for? The spouse, the children, or the grandparents? What types of promotions best speak to Hispanic shoppers?

The language dynamics and language spoken at home (Spanish, English, bilingual). For example, the shopper may be a Spanish-dominant adult, but she may want to please the children, who are probably bilingual and would enjoy products not advertised on Spanish-language media that they have tried at friends' homes. How can you use multiple media outlets to close these sales gaps?

The reason for the shopping trip. For example, is the trip "pay day" fun or a treat versus basic staples or weekend shopping with the whole family.

Specific store attributes. Is it just close to home? Or, can they find that specific nostalgic brand from "back home" in this particular store, or is it a store that offers product samples?

Their shopping experience. Are their expectations met at the store? Product assortment, fresh produce, value, trust, cleanliness, and respect are all considerations. Do they have a feel-good, welcoming experience when they patronize your store? "Can they speak my culture?" with kind, helpful, Spanish-speaking store associates and bi-lingual signage?

Immerse yourself in the Hispanic shopping environment

To be a successful supplier you need to partner with retailers that serve the Latino shopper. You need to be engaged with the retailers as well as their customers. A golden rule: I suggest that you spend a few days visiting different Hispanic neighborhoods in key Hispanic markets across the country. Walk the streets, talk to Latino shoppers, and understand where they go to shop and why. Look at the brands and product assortment in the stores in which they say they like to shop.

To deliver relevant programs you must be able to "walk in the shoes of the Hispanic shopper." An empathic approach will prove invaluable as you think through how to solve your consumer problems and develop your marketing and sales plans. Imagine you are an immigrant in a new city, with new brands, and with limited language skills. How would you manage?

Truly understanding local retail environments will show you the importance of smaller independent stores to Hispanic shoppers.

Locating smaller Hispanic stores

Unfortunately, finding smaller, Hispanic independent stores can prove to be challenging. However, you have some options. The local Hispanic Chambers of Commerce usually have a good list and can help make connections for you to build the first relationships. Local Hispanic newspapers also have a very good list of the Hispanic stores in their areas and can play a key role in reaching Latino cunsumers. Fortunately, independent retailer associations are emerging in Hispanic markets and they represent several of these stores. You can also contact national experts in Hispanic geo-segmentation and retailing strategies, like Geoscape, that probably know of most, if not all, Hispanic stores by zip codes. (See Chapter 4, *Geo-Segmentation Saves the Day.*)

Create your program

When suppliers and manufacturers are ready to partner with retailers, they must create and activate programs that drive Hispanic shoppers to the store. For example, sale circulars and coupons are distributed every week across the country. However, to get the desired response from the Hispanic shopper, these obviously need to be in-language and *in-culture.* What do I mean by in-culture? The circulars and coupons must highlight the product assortment Hispanics need and want, and must invite them to the store to get them. Our research shows that 83 percent of Hispanic shoppers check circulars for sales and coupons when they are planning a trip to the grocery store, 68 percent bring coupons from home, and 74 percent will pick up and use coupons that are available in-store.

Texting has come of age

Additionally, text messaging has become extremely popular among Latinos today and can bring Hispanic shoppers into your store. Texts that announce special sales or promotions can draw large response rates. With 75 percent of Hispanics now using cell phones on a regular basis, this is a fun new medium to invite Latino customers in a cultural way!

Product sampling is a good tactic

Eighty-six percent of Hispanic shoppers say that they try free product samples when offered in-store. We know from experience and research that free sampling activities are sometimes the only way Hispanics will try new or unfamiliar products. In-store sampling can also create a friendly, fun experience for the whole family, while building positive emotional associations with your brand.

Value packs are much appreciated

Because Hispanic moms are shopping for larger families, a multi-pack or large size value pack is always appreciated. It is also important to remember that many Hispanic households include teenage members, and we know they tend to consume their favorite foods in large quantities! Let your Latino shoppers know in the circulars that you offer these large family packs.

Strategically incorporate holidays

Holidays, and especially Hispanic holidays are loved and cherished celebration days in the Latino culture and it makes sense to incorporate them in your product promotions. Let's take a fictitious example of an Hispanic retail marketing plan, using Mother's Day and make it come alive. *El Dia de Las Madres* is a tribute to mothers and grandmothers, and like most Mediterranean families, traditional Latino culture goes overboard celebrating, recognizing and showing their appreciation and respect to "la Mama" and "la Abuelita!" To take advantage of the shopping that takes place to celebrate this special day, retailers will want to plan programs that reach the community in-culture. For example, use Hispanic radio or local Spanish-language newspapers or a mailer, and offer something that has special emotional meaning, like free flowers, or a coupon for a day of beauty, or a cake to share with all in the family. Latina moms give so much not only to their children and extended family, but also to others in the Latino community or the church. It means a great deal to honor her in a special and meaningful way. Therefore, it will pay to understand the meal occasions of *El Dia de Las Madres* and ensure that the promoted products are relevant for breakfast, lunch, dinner, and snacks for the celebrations that will take place all day long. This is a great opportunity for couponing as well.

Other specially powerful Hispanic holidays to consider include Lent/Easter; Hispanic Heritage Month (September/October); *El Dia de los Muertos*, Hispanic Halloween (November 1); and *Dia de los Reyes Magos*, Kings Day (January 6).

Make bold moves

Don't treat the Hispanic market like it is a small niche market. Be prepared to make some bold moves. Do more sampling than you would for the General Market. This promotional tactic can be expensive, but the long-term relationship you can build with your brand will make the investment worthwhile.

If you are doing in-store promotions, offer them in both Spanish and English. Think about it. Why does American Airlines and every other call center give callers a choice to speak in English or Spanish? Why are retailers still shy to make bold moves to bilingual or multi-lingual signage at the store?

Bringing it all together—the critical components:

- A good retailer and manufacturer partnership
- Culturally relevant insights
- Hispanic store segmentation and relevant product assortment
- Relevant shopper marketing and programming
- Building a connection with the community

The Partnership

It starts with a partnership. To successfully grow the Hispanic opportunity the retailer and the manufacturer must develop a trusting partnership built on candid communication and common goals. The manufacturer must build a trusting relationship for the long haul, with both the retailer and the community. This means manufacturers have to make a long-term commitment; this cannot be a program that is in-and-out once a year. A trusting relationship has to start with the manufacturer understanding factors like how important it is to have someone of like heritage making the sales calls. If we look at local retailers, we realize these stores are critical to the surrounding communities they serve. They provide employment opportunities. They have built their foundation on years of trust with the community, usually giving back to neighborhood schools and helping to prepare children to lead the generation of the future. How can a manufacturer help support that? The long-term relationship between the manufacturer and retailer will need to be transparent with respect to catering to the Hispanic consumer, shopper, and community at large. They will win together or lose together, but, based on my experience, if there is a partnership it will always be the former.

Culturally relevant insights

It takes time, funding, and commitment to truly understand the Hispanic market. C-Suite managers must get personally involved! You cannot just have your insights and marketing research teams conduct a few focus groups here and there and think you understand how to activate the store to win the Hispanic customer and retailer. You need to include multiple types of in-context research including in-home interviews, pantry-checks, shopalongs, market tours, and store manager interviews. Important: it is critical that senior level leaders also go out to tour the market so they get to know the shopper and the Hispanic independent stores first-hand! Reading a research report is not enough to truly understand what the authentic Hispanic retail experience is like—the tastes, the aromas, the feel, the sounds.

You need to know what Hispanic consumers have in their pantries. What are those spices and cultural flavors that contribute to a large share of the Hispanic household's "nostalgia" or culturally driven cuisine? How do they make their purchasing decisions? Where do they shop: supermarkets, local stores, drug stores, or mass market? How often do they shop? Which day of the week do they shop for which item? For example, do they shop for more produce and meat when these go on sale? If so, do they purchase large quantities to take advantage and freeze for later use? Do they pre-shop? We know Latino shoppers use coupons; however, we also know this varies by category. Hence, you need to find out the specifics for your product, or service, to turn these into powerful selling tools. Remember, the coupons usually live in the pantry of the shopper, reminding her (or him) of your brand and your store.

Hispanic store segmentation

Successfully classifying Hispanic stores is both an art and a science. We must use granular market data to understand not only the ethnicity of the shoppers in trade areas around the store, but also other culturally relevant demographic data, beyond their income levels. What are the shoppers' countries of origin and do their cultural backgrounds have an impact on the products and flavors they buy? What are the shopper preferences by store? It is fascinating to discover that even though most product categories are offered in all stores, Latino shoppers will drive long distances to different stores. Why? Maybe to find that special flavor or brand or value! The greater the granularity in understanding the multicultural consumer's preferences in specific zip codes, the greater the chances the product assortment in the stores will be right-on, in-culture, even within the same supermarket chain. The density of the Hispanic population in the store's zip code is certainly a relevant determining factor, although it is known Hispanic shoppers are willing to travel far for their favorite products, which can lead to varying shopping patterns in a tight geographical area. Therefore, information on shopping patterns needs to be incorporated in all in-culture insights retail studies.

At the end of the day, you'll want to partner with retailers to understand their store classification system or help them create one. Which stores are we classifying as "Hispanic" and what implications will that have on our product and promotion strategies?

The sales data challenge

Once we have a granular understanding of the shoppers' retail behavior we determine what drives the partnership perspective. It is an industry-wide issue that there are serious limitations in Hispanic retail sales data available today. Unfortunately, it makes it difficult to measure the success of Hispanic retail initiatives because all or most of the micro stores, convenience stores, and other Hispanic store formats are not included in most data sets of syndicated store data. Companies must rely on their primary research to "figure it out" and see how the Hispanic market sales meet the ROI and sales goals as well as how Hispanics are different or similar in their shopping habits and preferences from the non-Hispanic shopper. Sizing the retail opportunity, as well as planning and budgeting an in-culture retail strategy can be a costly and time consuming endeavor, and therefore not always easy.

The industry needs to find economical and efficient new ways to merge internal sales data with demographic retail data to confirm if the Latino initiative was successful, on an ROI basis, and also if a different strategy is needed to reach Hispanics.

Relevant shopper marketing

The in-store shopping experience is an especially critical component of Latino shopping. Therefore, shopper marketing strategies must be customized and funded appropriately to meet shoppers' expectations. There are many differences within the Hispanic market, from income to cultural background, that need to come alive in the shopping environment. Too many times the Hispanic shopping experience mirrors the General Market experience and there is no clear understanding of the store demographics and how much sales could increase if, for example, the unique Latino culture was highlighted in the store. From the large format stores to the micro-stores, the key is customization to truly reflect the neighborhood dynamics, the shopper dynamics, and to ensure that the experience is both pleasant and meaningful. Fortunately, with new in-culture tools and zip code based data this task is not as daunting as it once was.

Last but not least, all the great planning and customer insights in the world will not make up for the lack of an advertising agency that can deliver relevant and impactful messages in-culture. Manufacturers must make sure that their advertising agency has the capability and Hispanic cultural competence to deliver authentic programming to match the evolving market dynamics.

The best kept secret: Building connections with the community

Micro-store owners as well as large retail local managers can become Hispanic community "heroes." They know they impact the lives of the Latino shoppers in their stores as well as in the neighborhood. This is more so the case with the small Hispanic retail stores. Partnering with these small, yet critical retailers has the potential to positively impact not only the future of our country's communities, but your bottom line as well. They connect with Latino consumers one-on-one on a daily basis helping them build trust in brands, inviting them to actively participate in local community events, and encouraging them to take advantage of services like health clinics. Investing in local communities is a simple strategy, yet it can be easily misunderstood if manufacturers and retailers do not focus on building the relationship for the long term. Thinking of winning with Hispanic shoppers as a marathon and not a sprint will help your brand develop loyal Latino consumers and shoppers for life.

Be bold! This is no longer a *niche* market, this is **THE** Market!

PepsiCo is a world leader in convenient snacks, foods, and beverages and it is also a leader among companies with a strong commitment to an Hispanic strategy. *www.pepsico.com*

Building Latino Customer Relationships

Gabriela Alcántara-Diaz
President and Strategist, G ADMarketing Communications, Inc.

THIS CHAPTER takes a unique look at one of the fiercely competitive retail categories in a highly coveted region in the United States—the supermarket industry in South and Central Florida. Many of the lessons learned here are applicable to retailers and manufacturers that want to target highly developed categories within concentrated Hispanic markets.

Since the 1960s, the Hispanic community in Miami-Fort Lauderdale has been booming with waves of immigrants from the Caribbean, Central and South America. Orlando, on the other hand, is an emerging Hispanic market with immigrants from Puerto Rico as well as second and third generations of the same group relocating from Chicago and the Northeast.

With a high incidence of white-collar Hispanics, twice that of Los Angeles, South Florida represents an exceptionally desirable consumer segment. Unfortunately, there are no short cuts to dominating any category and the benefits of engaging a spectrum of Hispanic consumers well beyond short-term communication efforts, is essential for sustainable success.

As in other parts of the country, major retailers such as Walmart and, in the case of Florida, regional supermarket chains like Publix Super Markets, Winn-Dixie, and a handful of independent Hispanic grocery stores, such as Sedano's, employ long-term 360 retail branding strategies including:

- **Placement and saturation of multi-cultural stores**

  Designate stores based on three to five mile radius with Hispanic populations exceeding 40 percent throughout an entire DMA.

- **Potential in-culture store prototype**

  Cater exclusively to the Hispanic customer base with store brand formats, unique amenities, in-language services, pricing restructuring, reconfigured departments, and product SKU offerings, including opportunities to leverage brand equity through the retailer's ethnic private label line.

- **Re-merchandising of high incidence categories**

  Reset departments to reflect food categories that cater to the growing Hispanic consumer-base with SKUs, brands and packaging offering higher Hispanic sales potential, i.e., non-pre-packaged Meat/Seafood, Dairy, Deli, fresh Produce, Frozen and Bakery departments where services and product mix offering competes directly with Hispanic independent grocers and bodegas.

- **In-language employee hiring and in-culture customer service initiatives**

  Reflect the diversity of their local markets through trained, bilingual Hispanic employees delivering in-language services.

- **Targeted and differentiated marketing efforts**

  Integrate marketing communications efforts with a unique perspective on how Hispanic shoppers approach shopping trips, brand selections, and meal preparation.

Such efforts have guided these supermarket retailers to capitalize on the Hispanic segment's average grocery basket expenditure that is 10 percent higher in Miami than non-Hispanics' ($114 vs. $104), based on Experian Simmons 2010 data. This is consistent with Orlando's purchase patterns where Hispanic shoppers' expenditures average 7 percent higher than Non-Hispanics ($110 vs. $103). Overall, Latino purchases bring an incremental opportunity above $500 million annually.

	Miami				Orlando			
	2010		**2004**		**2010**		**2004**	
	Hispanic	Non-Hispanic	Hispanic	Non-Hispanic	Hispanic	Non-Hispanic	Hispanic	Non-Hispanic
Average customer expenditure per week	$114	$104	$111	$98	$110	$103	$101	$96
Index	110	100	113	100	107	100	105	100

Source: Experian Simmons 2010–Hispanic Grocery Expenditure, 2004–2010.

Developing Long-Term Loyalty

Let's explore what it takes to drive long-term loyalty and overall share of grocery basket expenditures among Hispanic shoppers. Many critical traits influence Latinos' brand and retailer preferences; therefore, it is important to recognize and address these in your strategic approach, while following four basic steps in marketing to Hispanic shoppers:

- **Employ** new product rollout approach*
- **Engage** Hispanic "Persona" in brand strategies*
- **Inspire** authentic communications*
- **Nurture** new brand experiences*

1. *Employ* a new product roll-out strategy

The basics are always the same. For example, when introducing a retail or product brand to the Hispanic consumer market, apply a new product rollout strategy similar to the one you might apply in the General Market, however, in-culture! Start by understanding the underpinnings of local Hispanic neighborhoods.

For example, when Publix launched its Publix Sabor stores in March 2005, the company was quoted in The Ledger.com, "It will be

---

*These phrases are copyrighted by Ms. Alcántara-Díaz and trademarks have been applied for.

an Hispanic supermarket with an Hispanic flavor. We're calling them Publix Sabor." Publix gained a leadership position in "being the first of the 10 largest traditional supermarkets chains to rollout an Hispanic-format supermarket," according to *Shopping Centers Today* in July 2006. With five Publix Sabor stores, Walmart and Winn-Dixie also stepped up their Hispanic customer efforts with in-store restaurant partnerships and re-merchandising programs with more Hispanic ethnic products and services. Walmart delivers an overall Cuban experience with its in-store dining through its partnership with Sergio's—local Hispanic-owned restaurants—serving up "empanadas, palomilla, and other signature Cuban dishes," according to the *Miami Herald*. Winn-Dixie's Hispanic strategy calls for "converting a number of its stores that are located in heavily Hispanic neighborhoods into a strictly Hispanic layout. The store expanded the number of perishables departments and added a Latino-influenced color scheme, in addition to bilingual signage," according to a report from Agri-Food Trade Service, *Marketing to Hispanic Consumers in the Southeast United States, February 2011*.

These retailers continue to create an in-culture shopping experience with Hispanic store formats, appealing departments, and product mix directed to an evolving, diverse, and price-sensitive Hispanic consumer-base.

2. *Engage* Hispanic "Persona" in brand strategies

As Hispanic communities continue to grow, there is a need to deeply connect and build relationships with the Hispanic Persona. To build these relationships, marketers need to understand the core elements of the Hispanic Persona that continue to be relevant across native and foreign-born Latinos alike. For instance, according to a study commissioned by the Association of Hispanic Advertising Agencies (AHAA), there are four pillars of the Latino identity:

Interpersonal Orientation

"Convivir" is to live, share life, to belong. It weaves in the positive feelings related to togetherness, camaraderie, and fellowship. Lasting connections to the Hispanic origin resonates throughout the communities and are seen in the camaraderie that develops within Hispanic communities, *familismo.*

Time and Space Perception

When it relates to time and space perception, socially, time tends to linger. Timeliness and firm schedules are often treated as flexible or general, but are also respected by those mindful of their "Americanized" gatherings among native-born Latinos. There is also a natural level of comfort, being physically close to others and living near family.

Spirituality

Knowing they are a part of a greater whole is a guiding force. Latino views are intangible and based on feelings. They are more fatalistic and identify more readily with nature ("It's God's Plan").

Gender

The Hispanic woman is the unifier who provides understanding, and creates balance in the family, whereas men embrace the evolution of a new way of life in the United States. While men are interested in sharing roles, a certain level of "traditional" gender role is still expected and found among more traditional Hispanic families.

3. *Inspire* and discover authentic communications

Inspiring Latinos with authenticity takes a lot more than communicating in-language; it takes understanding and appealing to their diversity. And this can vary within the Hispanic market. For example, Cuban Hispanics tend to be more open-minded, experimental, and receptive, and more open to new experiences. On the other hand, Mexican Latinos can present the opposite traits, less inclined to be experimental, learn by "wait and see" from close personal and family networks, be more risk averse and slow to adopt new foods or beverage products. More acculturated and young Mexicans and Cubans may transcend traditional ethnic values and exhibit multi-dimensional beliefs. (M. I. Valdés, 1992 and 2007) These are insights to consider when developing your communication strategy.

Engaging an Hispanic market segment requires broad and in-depth ethnographies that can reflect the evolved Hispanic household with blended cultures, having complex ideals, and varied aspirations.

Despite the South Florida market's economic complexity and continuous expansion by Walmart with a total of nine stores and two additional locations planned in Miami-Dade, the leading retailer, Publix, continues to benefit from continuous increases in share of Spanish-dominant, loyal shoppers. According to Experian Simmons data, 32 percent of Miami's Spanish-dominant shoppers shopped at Publix four or more times in 2010 in the four weeks before the survey, a "loyalty" increase of 5 share points from 2004. Similarly, Orlando's data also reflects an increase of 5 share points among loyal shoppers to 26 percent in 2010, coming mostly at the expense of Winn-Dixie's Spanish-dominant base. Walmart was also successful growing its loyal base (4+ times in "last month") among Spanish-dominants, achieving only a modest increase (+2 points) in Miami and a sharp jump (+14 points) in Orlando. Similarly, Publix shows success in expanding its base among more affluent Latinos, gaining seven share points among households in Miami with annual incomes of $25,000 to $75,000; four of these points came from Winn-Dixie.

The Experian Simmons report explained, "Publix's multi-ethnic communications and retail efforts continue to solidify their base lead against all three retailers in overall shopping by Hispanics in the past 4 weeks, despite Walmart's low-price positioning, especially in Orlando."

How did they do it? By having an honest, authentic dialogue with Hispanic consumers.

4. *Nurture* new brand experiences

Hispanics, not only the Spanish-dominant but also the first generation born in the United States, may not be immersed in all levels and facets of mainstream American culture and society. This is due principally to a lack of exposure. When marketers recognize this and provide Latino customers the respectful nurturing necessary to become familiar with "new" benefits and show them how to use a "new" brand, chances are it will become a game changer. For example, strategies such as in-store sampling, or educational couponing, fliers, branded magazines, or ads, that describe the new product in-culture, help the product adoption process to move more quickly.

Bilingual retail programs and tailored product promotions do very well too, as Hispanic shoppers are heavily influenced by in-store promotions. According to *Multicultural View: Multicultural Women Shopper Insights*, the 2010 Yankelovich MONITOR Multicultural Marketing Study, when compared with their General Market counterparts Latinos are six times more likely to try or buy a new product if they are given an in-store demonstration. Yet, this is only the price of entry into the Hispanic nucleus.

As marketers continue their quest for a larger share of the Hispanic grocery basket, at least five attributes continue to be crucial when driving Latino shopping consideration:

- Reasonable prices and convenience
- Hispanic or Hispanic-friendly employees (considered important by 47 percent of Latinos vs. 16 percent of the General Market)
- Outstanding customer service, including Spanish-speaking and knowledgeable customer service and salespeople
- Displaying bilingual signage (more important to Spanish-dominant Hispanics)
- High-quality Hispanic produce and product items, ideally from diverse Latin American countries

Cultivating relationships with Latino shoppers is a long-term commitment that requires a comprehensive and effective marketing approach and long-term financial investment. Latino customers, in turn, will become your brand ambassadors and a main component of your retail base growth.

G ADMarketing Communications is a strategic marketing consultancy firm that specializes in aligning brands with today's evolved Hispanic consumer. The company provides strategic guidance to marketers focusing on engaging and catering to the needs of the affluent and middle-class Hispanic segments. *www.gadmarketingcomm.com*

The Best Kept Secret:
Authentic Hispanic Supermarkets

Don Longo
Editorial Director, Stagnito Media, Hispanic Retail 360 Summit

I'VE BEEN managing the content for the Hispanic Retail 360 Summit, the largest gathering of retailers and consumer product goods (CPG) firms targeting the growing Hispanic population, for the past seven years. During that time, I've heard many great companies—from PepsiCo to Procter & Gamble, Coca-Cola to Kraft—talk about and demonstrate their robust marketing plans to increase their business with Hispanic shoppers. They've described how they target and segment Latino shoppers; how they align their products with specific customer segments; and how they identify and exploit key lifestyle and emotional touch points with the Hispanic consumer, such as specific campaigns around soccer or the importance of family.

However, what seems to be missing from many marketing plans of the big CPG companies is an appreciation of the important role of the authentic Hispanic retailer.

These independent companies exist all over the U.S. but are mainly concentrated in California, Nevada, New Mexico, Arizona, Texas, Florida and some large metropolitan areas, such as New York and Chicago. Not counting General Market chains with strong multicultural appeal, such as Texas-based H.E.B., there are several thousand of what I call authentic Hispanic supermarkets throughout the country, from small chains to mom-and-pop stores. Nearly every Hispanic neighborhood has at least one traditional supermarket, in addition to several bodegas.

Perhaps it's because of the lack of syndicated data from these independents (whose sales are not generally accounted for by researchers like Nielsen and IRI), but

CPG companies typically do not have the same relationship with authentic Hispanic retailers that they have with more mainstream supermarkets. For one thing, Hispanic supermarkets attract a very different customer than the mainstream players.

A recent study of the Dallas/Fort Worth market by Rincon & Associates found that while 25.4 percent of all Hispanics in the market said they bought the majority of their groceries at a Walmart Supercenter, authentic Hispanic grocers like Fiesta Mart (29.4 percent) and El Rancho (11.1 percent) were the first and third choices among foreign-born Hispanics. Walmart Supercenter's percentage dropped to 21.8 percent among foreign-born Hispanics.

In addition to the customer base, the profit structure of Hispanic supermarkets is different than that of mainstream retailers, according to a recent cover story by *Hispanic Retail 360* magazine. Most Latino chains generate super high turns in fresh food. At Mi Pueblo Food Centers in northern California, fresh food comprises more than 50 percent of its offerings; usually, it is the other way around for conventional grocers. Many Hispanic supermarkets are smaller in size than mainstream ones and their center store offerings are limited. But many Hispanic chains take lower center store margins and recoup lost profits via rapid turns of their fresh foods.

Even mainstream retailers that have expanded their Hispanic offerings don't sell the breadth and depth of authentic products that Hispanic retailers carry. Sylmar, California based Vallarta Supermarkets' product mix is broader than Walmart's and it makes its own tortillas. It also has a taqueria in every location with tables for in-store dining. Other Hispanic supermarkets have "from scratch" restaurants and bakeries as well.

Most Latino supermarkets offer special services like check cashing, bill payment, and wire transfers. Some also have pharmacies, cell phone kiosks, and even rent-to-own appliance centers. These add-on businesses are often aimed at Latinos who lack credit or bank accounts.

Many authentic Hispanic supermarkets share similar complaints about CPG companies concerning the timeliness of delivery, package sizes, and product mix. Because they are smaller than the major companies like Kroger and Albertsons, they are more dependent on wholesalers for their product needs.

At the same time, they do give credit where credit is due. One manager of an Hispanic supermarket said that online recipes from CPG companies like General Mills and Kraft really drive sales at the store.

Juvenal Chavez, founder of Mi Pueblo Food Centers, offered one final piece of advice for CPG companies: Despite the growing U.S. Hispanic population, his clientele, like that of other authentic Hispanic retailers, is changing. While the core customer base is still first-generation Latinos, he now counts growing numbers of "more acculturated," second- and third-generation Latinos of Mexican heritage, more Central and South Americans, and even more Anglos as the tastes of the Latino "majority-minority" become fused with the new mainstream.

Stagnito Media plays a leadership role in providing market data, case studies and networking opportunities to the retail community through its Hispanic Retail 360 Summit and *Hispanic Retail 360* magazine. Don Longo is editorial director. Hispanic Retail 360 has access to the thought leaders in the Hispanic marketing field and understands the major issues faced by retailers trying to grow their business with the Hispanic population. *Convenience Store News* and *Progressive Grocer* magazines provide Stagnito with audience reach into the supermarket and convenience store industries, along with the consumer product goods companies that serve those industries.

21st Century Segmentation for a Multi-dimensional Consumer

César M. Melgoza
Founder & CEO, Geoscape

Why Segmentation Matters

With over 315 million people and 52 million Latinos in America, and 3.7 million more in Puerto Rico, segmentation is often necessary to ensure that products are relevant, messages resonate, and the business strategy makes the best use of precious corporate resources. Segmenting the Latino population shares common objectives and techniques, yet important distinctions exist across a spectrum of attributes such as language, buying potential, lifestage, lifestyle, country of origin, attitudes, and emotional connections. Most marketers realize that segmentation is important for their business strategy. However too many are unable to execute specific Latino strategies and tactics that enable them to put segmentation into practice. The most common segmentation platforms develop descriptions of consumer types that are insightful and help guide a high-level strategy, but are insufficient to meet the demands of specific operational needs. The days of mass marketing have come and gone, and micro (small group) and nano (individual) targeting is required to effectively motivate consumers to desire and purchase your brands.

Are Common Practices, "Best Practices"?

The velocity of our economy is made possible by the combination of modern communications technology and the media. In the age of "now," consumers expect to communicate as well as purchase at the speed of light—through e-commerce. New channels of communication and buying are giving way to new methods of understanding consumers and their preferences and the trade-offs between things like brand, price, and packaging.

There is a lot to know, and unfortunately we cannot be experts on every subject of importance, nor do we have the time. Furthermore, the rate of turnover in American corporations also makes it challenging to retain institutional knowledge that is essential in building a long-term understanding of consumer behavior.

Today's common practices may not be "best practices" either. Understanding what best practices are today requires a multi-disciplinary approach to market intelligence. Most practitioners in the field use the term "market research," which is broad and somewhat vague. I prefer the term market intelligence to depict the variety of disciplines required to develop a multi-dimensional and actionable understanding of consumers. Market intelligence includes both primary and secondary research as well as demographics, statistical analysis, and geographic or spatial analysis.

In the 21st-century multi-cultural marketplace, all these disciplines are required to enable a truly actionable segmentation system. You may be thinking that this is a heavy requirement and perhaps not always necessary and that is sometimes correct. For basic, rapid segmentation, or to enhance what you already know about your customer base, you may not need to dive deep into these methods. Sometimes a "pre-built" system with quickly defined composite segmentation may be sufficient. You can then use building blocks that have been prepared for you to develop a long term and more robust segmentation platform. However, for those who want to take their Hispanic, African-American, or Asian strategy and its investment to another level, a deep and custom segmentation platform may be the way to go and the means to build a company wide marketing knowledge asset.

Figure 1 illustrates the range of options for consumer segmentation— some quick and relatively superficial and others deep and demanding. The good news is that with today's technology and data resources, it is possible to produce very sophisticated segmentation platforms well within a budget cycle. Let me describe each of the segmentation building blocks specifically.

Figure 1. *Options for Consumer Segmentation*

Demographic and Economic Databases

Spatial (Geographic) Analysis and Visualization

Qualitative Research

Quantitative Research

Conjoint Analytics/Trade-off Modeling

Behavioral Measurement

Psychographic/Attitudinal/Emotion Testing

Need-state Modeling

Ground-Truth® Segment Enumeration: Individuals, Households

Deployment on Strategy

Deployment on Operations: product, distribution, staffing, experience

Deployment on Media: placement and messaging

Adding In-Culture to demographic and economic databases

Incorporating demographic and economic characteristics is fundamental to segmentation. These data are most commonly acquired from the Census Bureau—both from the decennial census and the ongoing annual *American Community Survey.* The Census Bureau offers a wealth of resources including data on demographic and economic data by ethnicity and race as well as other dimensions. Many of these data sets are available directly from their website and are often integrated into publications by third party organizations.

Marketers who need and want more up-to-date and value-added

demographic and economic data should consider acquiring current year and forecasted geo-demographic and economic data from a commercial supplier. These suppliers use the census plus additional modeling, research, and data hygiene techniques to expand, and improve data resources published by the Census Bureau. Additionally, these suppliers make the data available by regions not offered by the Bureau such as zip codes and DMAs (Nielsen's Designated Market Areas) and other specialized geographic coverage areas.

Geoscape® supplies its data by nine standard geographic areas and invests a great deal of energy and time into enhancing and extending census demographic and economic data—especially the cultural elements related to Hispanic, Asian, and other high-growth cultural segments.

We created American Marketscape DataStream™ (AMDS)

The American Marketscape DataStream (AMDS) is a product that includes current year population and household estimates and 5-year projections on a plethora of metrics that enable marketers to run analysis from the nation as a whole down to the individual block level. The AMDS also includes specialized in-culture metrics on elements such as:

- *Acculturation:* Hispanicity™ and Asianicity™
- *Language Use:* For Hispanic and several Asian languages
- *Localized Income:* Household Income Indices calibrated to the local population
- *Socioeconomic Strata:* Incorporating various personal and household characteristics
- *Technology Adoption:* Indices comparing geographic areas and population groups
- *Consumer Spending:* Across categories of products and services

Figure 2 shows a summary of the techniques and outputs used for the AMDS data creation included in these in-culture products.

Figure 2 *Summary of techniques and outputs used for data creation in the in-culture products*

Macro-to-micro coverage	In-depth representation of U.S. cultural diversity	Over 1,500 indicators on various subject areas
U.S., state, Nielsen Designated Market Area (DMA), metro area, country, congressional district, zip code, census tract, and block group levels	Employs proprietary household & individual data Uses proprietary DirecTarget® Technology Incorporates dozens of public and private source data sets including primary research surveys	Identifies cultural population missed by the census and helps to rectify the under-count in recent immigrant groups Includes building permit & residential build-out data Language, income, age cohorts, socioeconomic status (SES), country of origin, consumer spending, acculturation, technology adoption and many others
Built from the ground up by a specialized team		Features 337 detailed consumer spending Dynamix™ (CSDX) by major ethic group plus 15 major category and 4 summary variables

Source: GeoScape

Acculturation and the Hispanicity Framework

Acculturation has long been a familiar framework for analysis and segmentation of Hispanic consumers. As opposed to assimilation, where individuals shed their original heritage to acquire a new (American) culture, acculturation connotes the process where migrants and their offspring retain key elements of their original culture while acquiring components of the American culture. (M.I. Valdés, 1992) Some marketers in the Hispanic space seem to want to dismiss the importance of acculturation and may be eager to

Multi-dimensional Hispanicity

Acculturation

Socioeconomic strata

Country of origin

Psychographics

Language use

Buying power

Lifestage

Media & shopping behavior

find alternatives. I believe they miss the point, which is that acculturation is a necessary and important factor, but certainly not the only element important to sound segmentation approaches. Therefore, acculturation plus other important dimensions will continue to provide decision value, even as the U.S. Hispanic population acculturates into an increasingly bi-cultural population.

Geoscape produced the Hispanicity framework to define Hispanics across key segments and enable their enumeration geographically and within a database of individuals.

Figure 3 *Acculturation: Hispanicity™ CultureCodes®*

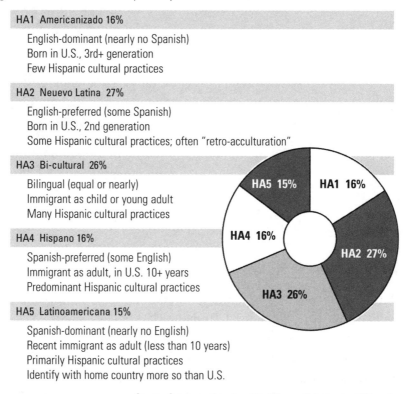

HA1 Americanizado 16%

English-dominant (nearly no Spanish)
Born in U.S., 3rd+ generation
Few Hispanic cultural practices

HA2 Neuevo Latina 27%

English-preferred (some Spanish)
Born in U.S., 2nd generation
Some Hispanic cultural practices; often "retro-acculturation"

HA3 Bi-cultural 26%

Bilingual (equal or nearly)
Immigrant as child or young adult
Many Hispanic cultural practices

HA4 Hispano 16%

Spanish-preferred (some English)
Immigrant as adult, in U.S. 10+ years
Predominant Hispanic cultural practices

HA5 Latinoamericana 15%

Spanish-dominant (nearly no English)
Recent immigrant as adult (less than 10 years)
Primarily Hispanic cultural practices
Identify with home country more so than U.S.

Source: Geoscape: American Marketscape Datastream, 2011 series

Figure 3 shows the overall nationwide distribution of Hispanics by Hispanicity acculturation segments and various dimensions of consumer behavior, demographics, lifestyles, and emotions. We can also map these groups across geographic areas either separately by each segment or in combination with another key element, such as socioeconomic status. Maps can reveal the neighborhoods (block groups and zip codes) where unacculturated, upper-class Latinos live by density (percentage). For example in Miami, some of the areas are generally known, but even long-term residents will find new pockets of opportunity they may not have been aware of when they see the groups mapped.

Spatial or Geographic Analysis

Viewing data across a geographic area is helpful for both understanding the exact physical location and distribution of your multi-cultural consumers and anticipating their shopping and media behavior. As the saying goes, "a picture is worth a thousand words" because images can easily impart information that words alone cannot. Spatial or geographic analysis often involves what is known as "thematic mapping." Some marketers these days prefer to use the term "heat mapping" or some other cool name that will entice you to pay attention. Essentially, thematic mapping refers to the linkage of data with geographic areas, and then expressing the data by a color, shade, or symbol that can reveal patterns in the information. For example, Figure 4 shows the distribution of the U.S. Hispanic population

Figure 4 *Thematic Map, Hispanic Population Distribution in the U.S.*

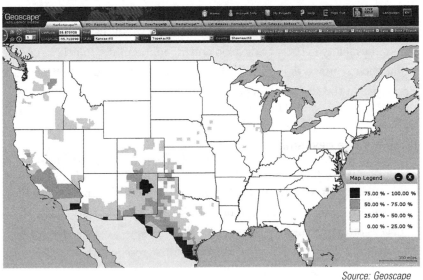

Source: Geoscape

in 2016 by county across the nation. The image tells us that although the Hispanic population will continue to show higher concentration in the Southwest in 2016, many places will now be home to a significant proportion of Hispanics. However, decades ago the Hispanic population was concentrated in a region and not as expansive.

Qualitative Research

The need to measure consumer insights and characteristics that are difficult to quantify is what inspires qualitative research such as "focus groups" or "ethnography" or other qualitative methodology. When speaking of "common practices vs. best practices" some marketers note that often limited attention is placed on the sampling method for selecting focus group participants. For expediency, and perhaps costs, most local research facilities offer their own lists of able and willing participants who normally receive a fee for their participation in the focus groups. Nonetheless, the savvy marketer will want to ensure that those people selected represent a good proportionate cross-section of the consumer segment being studied. This requires analytics based on the overall market segments' populations and proportions based on key characteristics like language, country-of-origin, lifestage, socioeconomic strata, gender, product, media usage, and acculturation level. A representative, well-balanced recommended approach should pull from a broad universe within a reasonable distance from the facility in order to develop and fill an in-culture matrix to ensure that each segment is represented to a reasonable degree based on their presence in the study area's population.

Quantitative Research

Quantitative research is the term generally used for large population or survey research studies, conducted through a variety of means, the most common of which are telephone surveys, door-to-door studies, mailed surveys or diaries, public intercepts, online surveys, and panels.

There are numerous aspects of quantitative research that require deep cultural insights, category, brand and marketplace knowledge. However, the area that often falls short is the sampling design. A fundamental step in sampling design is ensuring that participating respondents are proportionate to the *universe* being studied.

For example, if you survey the Hispanic population and language preference is an important factor, as it normally is, then you'll want to ensure that a proportionate number of respondents are secured from each major language preference group. The geographic region being studied also matters. If the study is national, then national proportions should be adhered to, but if the sample is state-wide or regional it requires different proportions. Sometimes over-sampling is needed to help to achieve more accurate results. When an insufficient number of respondents from a particular group are interviewed, statistical weighting can partially offset the shortcomings of the collected data. However, there are limitations to this statistical technique of which you need to be aware. You cannot extrapolate and derive marketing conclusions to an entire city or state, from a miniscule consumer segment sample. For example, a study or database that includes only 10 non-acculturated Latinos, or 5 single women, does not have the statistical weight or power to represent the entire population of non-acculturated Latinos or Latinas. Sadly, this is a failing of many large syndicated data suppliers. I have to encourage you to ask your research vendor or data provider to give you the actual break downs of the Hispanic socio, cultural, and psychographic characteristics and request that the money you are paying for their data is actually giving you reliable results. These research concerns and others are discussed in greater detail in the two research chapters that follow. (See Chapter 6, Hispanic Marketing Research.)

Wording makes a difference!

Wording each study question with care is fundamental. I often see surveys that include the terminology "Spanish Only" and "English Only." Whereas this may seem rational on the surface, the study participant may interpret the question differently than the researcher. As the body of research on this specific subject shows (see studies by, for example, Professor Fedrico Subervi, PhD) Latinos can switch their language use considerably depending on the social occasion or the location where they are interacting and if people who speak only English are present. Therefore, unless questions are added that specifically probe for these factors, survey study responses can paint a picture that misrepresents what is truly happening in the marketplace. For example, a response that allows only one language will tend to make this group smaller, since countless studies show that in nearly all Hispanic households some English or Spanish is spoken at least some of the time and not just one language or the other. Based on these insights, at Geoscape, we use the following language categories for language segmentation purposes. The percentages show the national distribution, although the mix of segments varies by region and metro area.

English-dependent	22 percent
Bilingual, English-preferred	27 percent
Bilingual, Equal	13 percent
Bilingual, Spanish-preferred	18 percent
Spanish dependent	20 percent

As you can see, the majority of the Hispanic population is bilingual to some degree with about 20 percent being dependent on either language. Although Spanish Language Use is but one attribute, it is often a key building block within a segmentation platform. It also can and should be extended into the context of language use, such as at home, at work, or when shopping, whenever appropriate.

Conjoint or Trade-off Analysis

A powerful technique that can be incorporated into a segmentation platform is known as conjoint analysis, which is a technique whereby consumers are asked to decide between competing attributes of a product or service. This technique is most commonly used for pricing studies but also can be applied to the effects of brand messaging, offers, packaging, or channel of purchase. Conjoint studies normally are performed within a questionnaire framework, although they can be executed in a focus group format. The mathematics involved are somewhat advanced and these days software programs exist to facilitate the generation of results.

A Case Study: Wireless Communications

Geoscape built an in-culture segmentation platform for a wireless telecommunications supplier where we incorporated conjoint techniques across a variety of customer segments. The comparisons included pricing for both handsets and use plans along with competing brands and other key marketing elements. This process enabled us to link these attributes to each segment and therefore create compelling differentiators between segments that resulted in actionable levers, such as modifying offers and promotions for the different segments based on these tradeoffs. Furthermore, these segments were linked to individual customers and to prospects throughout the nation so that Geoscape's model could simulate demand ubiquitously, including classification of store trade areas to the point that in-store promotions could be tailored to the surrounding population. These granular in-culture marketing directives saved our client the cost of targeting customers with the incorrect offering and allowed the client to dramatically increase its sales!

Behavioral Measurement

Measuring actual consumer behavior—as opposed to self-reported preferences from a survey or focus group—is another powerful segmentation building block. Behavior is most commonly measured today via purchase transaction data. When linked to an individual or household, transaction based behavioral data can yield powerful facts and trends about specific consumer groups and can contribute key elements to a segmentation platform.

A powerful and current example of the use of behavioral data is the linkage of grocery shopping transactions from loyalty card member data. Recently, Dunnhumby and Geoscape collaborated to code Kroger's loyalty file in order to identify Hispanic cardholders' acculturation levels (Hispanicity™ segment). The cardholders were identified and coded using Geoscape's DirecTarget® SDK which is a server-based database enrichment technology that adds ethnicity, race, country-of-origin, gender, and religious preference to any file containing a name and address. The result of this process is the ability to link millions of consumers by ethnicity and acculturation level and myriad transaction-based behaviors. These data are embedded within an online reporting platform offered by Dunnhumby, known as *The Shop*, where data can be analyzed and visualized to reveal patterns in consumption of products cross-tabbed by date, time, offer, price, and other powerful business and marketing dimensions. This capability provides robust in-culture decision support across consumer types, including the burgeoning Hispanic market.

For example, detailed shopping behavior data can reveal tangible facts about Hispanic consumer preferences across the acculturation spectrum. One of our studies found that unacculturated buyers are clearly more likely to purchase multiple flavors of the same product compared with their bi-cultural and acculturated counterparts.

Psychographic, Attitudinal, and Emotional Factors

Consumer psychological characteristics are powerful marketing variables, yet often elude the grasp of marketers. Furthermore, linking psychological aspects to tangible demographic and cultural factors has until recently been difficult to incorporate into Hispanic marketing data products. Many of these characteristics are associated with one or more distinct personal attributes and therein lies the power of linking psychographic, attitudinal, and emotional factors into a segmentation platform.

For example, when observing attitudes about the use of financial services such as loans by Hispanic households across acculturation segments, it becomes clear that such use is directly correlated with the acculturation process. For example, we cross-tabbed Hispanicity segments by the concept of whether or not borrowing money makes Latino consumers "feel uncomfortable," a relationship that may be surprising. Less-acculturated Hispanics appeared less *uncomfortable* borrowing money than those who are fully acculturated. Deep Latino consumer marketing insights are easily available. For example, syndicated survey data from GfK Mediamark is linked to Geoscape Hispanicity database within the online Geoscape Intelligence System and these provide compelling insights within minutes.

Need-state Modeling

Need-state modeling is yet another powerful form for understanding how consumer segments can respond to brands and offers. A combination of pragmatism and emotions is at play, depending on the product and circumstances. Categories such as alcoholic beverages have used this method effectively to enable segmentation by consumer types as well as by business establishment. For example, a person "needing" to unwind after a hard day's work could frequent a bar or pub as opposed to picking up a twelve-pack on the way home. Another person's need to unwind could be intertwined with the need to interact with others in a social setting, therefore increasing the relevance of the pub, bar, or happy hour.

Need-state modeling normally is performed via conjoint and/or qualitative research—where consumer behaviors, preferences, and so on, are uncovered—and then these are linked to consumer types. This type of analysis is closely associated with psychographic, attitudinal, and emotional elements discussed in the prior section, but it specifically addresses product use and timing. Again, these are new tools now available to target the Hispanic market, in-culture.

All in one place: Ground-Truth Segmentation®

The concept of Ground-Truth segmentation was developed by Geoscape over the past decade after experiencing a full range of segmentation techniques and approaches, many of which did not link explicitly to individual consumers and households. This technique enables the linkage of qualitative and quantitative data to actual customers and prospects via advanced database, statistical, and spatial analytics. The result is improved practicality as the segments become actionable across strategy, creative guidance, product planning, distribution, and media selection.

Figure 5 *Segmentation Approaches*

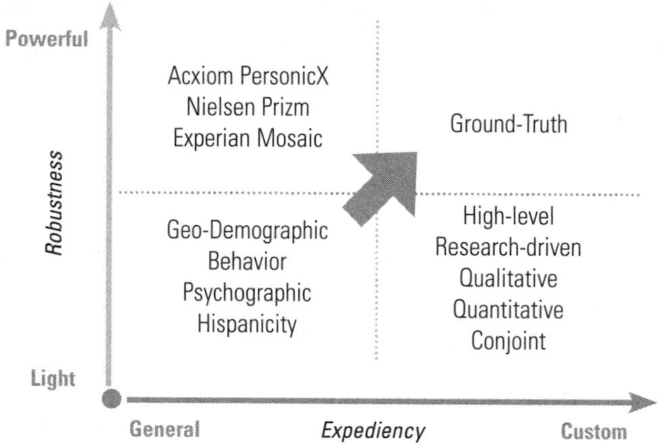

A Case Study: Health Insurance

A health insurance company seeks to define key segments across channels and insurance plan types. Socio-demographics as well as psychographics are incorporated in the analysis, as well as cultural and acculturation elements. The insurance company is attempting to drive strategy and priorities, and deploy marketing options towards specific potential policyholders and benefits such as pharmaceutical coverage. The beauty and power of Ground-Truth Segmentation is that it provides both the topline business and marketing guidance and the precise measurement to all stakeholders, consumers, prospects, retailers, and media coverage options.

Pre-built Consumer Segmentation Systems

For want of a better term, "pre-built" or off-the-shelf segmentation systems have been available for decades. They typically combine demographic and lifestyle characteristics into a matrix of segments and sub-segments that can be enumerated and linked through syndicated research to consumer preference of a variety of products, categories, media and other outcomes. Among the pre-built segmentation systems available today is PersonicX™ by Acxiom,® which is available for both Classic and Hispanic editions. These segments can be linked to direct marketing lists as well as to geographic areas, which can then be linked to other regions such as store trade areas and media coverage.

Continuing with the health insurance case study, Personicx™ can be used to identify a specific Hispanic composite or special sub-segments along with their residential settlement patterns and proximity to retail outlets.

The Pre-built Segmentation approach is often expedient and powerful, although it can lack the specificity of a custom approach built for a specific company. The use of these systems can be effective and requires a far lower investment of both budget and time to implement.

Summary

In-culture, intelligent consumer segmentation is a key requirement for marketers who must ensure they leverage their budget and opportunities to the maximum in the current business and retail marketplace. This likely includes all readers of this book. Fortunately, thanks to the data provided by the U.S. Census Bureau, other public resources as well as proprietary research and modeling along with the ever-increasing power of computer technology, in-culture consumer segmentations are not only efficient, powerful, and insightful but also economic and accessible to businesses of all sizes. Figure 6 (page 70), as an example, shows a summary of the available choices for consumer segmentation in heathcare. The fact that the most advanced segmentation approaches now offer a wealth of dimensions for Hispanic consumers is great news for marketers endeavoring to tap the *New American Mainstream* consumer and today's *Growth-Majority* where Latino individuals and households are prominent.

Anyone desiring to explore these subjects further is invited to contact me personally at cmelgoza@geoscape.com or 1-888-211-9353.

Via its U.S. headquarters in Miami and its European base in Amsterdam, **Geoscape** provides strategic guidance, technology-fueled data products and analytic services. The Geoscape Intelligence System (GIS), the DirecTarget® database enrichment system, American Marketscape DataStream™ geo-demographics and a variety of other databases and technologies are deployed successfully by hundreds of corporations. Geoscape produces and hosts the annual New American Mainstream Business Summit. *www.geoscape.com*

Figure 6 *Ground-Truth Segment Matrix*

1. No health care	2. Employer-sponsored health care	3. Individually purchased health care
1A. Single and Young	2A. Single or independent coverage	3A. Lowest cost option or partial coverage
May live in parent's home, don't see the immediate need for health care. Employer may offer coverage, but elect not to participate in plan.	Adults with individual coverage. Students using plans provided by colleges or universities.	Individuals and families with limited income or looking for lowest priced option. Includes SCHIP and Medicaid participants.
Ages 18–35 (main group 18–24)	Ages 18–65 (main group 21–35)	All ages
Lower income (either low personal income when living with parents or low household income when living in separate dwelling) SES C-E	SES A-C	SES C-E
Little or no credit history	Some college or higher	Mostly renters
1B Low-income families	**2B Family plans**	**3B. Value shoppers**
Lower income (low personal income, low household income, or unemployed), if employed, coverage is not offered or not affordable.	Families sharing coverage, primarily married couples with children at home	Value driven individuals and families, research health plans prior to making choice. Some are opt-out from employer coverage for increased value.
Ages 21–60 (main group 25-50)	Ages 23–65 (main group 25–55)	Ages 25–65 (main group 25–55)
SES D-E	SES A-D	SES B-C
Children at home	Children at home	Some college or higher
Mostly renters	Mostly home owners	
1C Fixed income	**2C Retired**	**3C Medicare**
Older adults, no longer covered or unable to afford coverage.	Families or individuals with older or grown children. Opt to continue employer coverage in retirement.	Older single or married couples, retired, enrolled in Medicare.
Aged 60+	Ages 55+ (main group 65+)	Ages 50+ (main group 65+)
SES D-E	SES A-C	SES B-D

Hispanic Audience Measurement Today

Douglas Darfield

SVP Multicultural Measurement, Nielsen Media Research

ALTHOUGH Hispanics have been present in sizable numbers in the United States since the early days of the Republic, the modern history of measurement of Hispanics in the U.S. really begins with the 1980 U.S. Census. That year, a question on Hispanic descent or origin was added to the census short form in a manner that clearly separated Hispanic identity from the issue of race. Since that time, the emergence of Hispanics as the primary driver of demographic and ethnographic change throughout the country has had a profound impact on many aspects of American life.

2012 is the 20th anniversary of another important milestone for Hispanic measurement. While the census over the years has provided a clear call to action in terms of why it is important for marketers to understand how to reach Hispanics, the 1992 introduction of the Nielsen Hispanic Television Index (NHTI) provided, for the first time, a truly comprehensive view of how Hispanics consumed major media in ongoing syndicated research. Today, much of the research that undergirds Hispanic marketing in the U.S. is based on the work on television audience measurement that began at Nielsen 20 years ago.

While much good work had been conducted by smaller independent research firms in the Hispanic market, before the beginning of the Nielsen Hispanic Television Index (NHTI) service, the large syndicated companies had, for the most part, steered clear of the area. Nielsen had been making its viewing or listening diaries available in Spanish since the 1980s, but for the most part there was not a strong focus on recruiting Spanish-dominant Hispanics, nor was there an awareness of the impact on audience estimates of not doing so. On the flip side, Spanish-language media, the television industry in particular, had developed alternative data sources. They concentrated on contacting Spanish speakers, in most cases to the exclusion of anyone else. Thus, you had one group of sources that implied that Hispanics were found in sufficient numbers using English-language media and that no special efforts were required, whereas a second group of sources claimed that virtually no Hispanics ever spoke English, much less watched English-language TV. Taken altogether the lack of clear, reliable data resulted in a resounding call to inaction to confused marketers.

Recognizing that the existing situation was a clear impediment to growth, Univision and Telemundo joined together as the Spanish Television Research Committee to try to break through the logjam. Proposals were requested from many different companies, but in the end the committee decided to work with Nielsen to develop a comprehensive television measurement in which all segments of the Hispanic market were represented fairly and fully in the audience reporting sample.

Creating the sample

Faced with the task of creating the new service, Nielsen first surveyed the resources available to do the job. The core of Nielsen's work in measuring television in the U.S. is a strong conviction that a good random area probability sample with a high cooperation rate is the best way to ensure full and fair audience measurement. That being said, there is recognition that differential response rates (the likelihood that certain segments of the population are more likely to participate in research then others) may affect the representatives of the installed sample. In order to mitigate the effects of differential response rates, Nielsen "forces a match" on certain household characteristics between a refusing basic and the alternate that is eventually installed to take its place. In the General Market, the characteristics most closely aligned with viewing were (and still are) cable and satellite penetration and presence of children. When looking at the Hispanic market, while those characteristics were important, it was obvious that something more was needed to guarantee accurate representation of both Spanish-language and English-language television viewers.

The importance of language

Language was the obvious place to start. It was assumed that in some way language use levels had to be accounted for in order to correctly apportion Hispanic viewing between Spanish- and English-language television. At the time when this was being done, there were many alternative questions about language use being explored throughout the Hispanic marketing community. To begin with, there was the basic census question that asked people what languages they spoke. Use of the census model would have had the advantage of clarity and simplicity, but the lack of a clear measure of levels of usage beyond simple comprehension in the census question led Nielsen to consider going a bit further. Going back to first principles, which in this case is that Nielsen measures television viewing in the home, the logical approach to take was to develop an accurate measure of what language Hispanics were speaking in their homes and then to develop an overall methodology that reflected those results in the installed sample.

In order to develop a Universe Estimate for language use in the home that was of sufficient rigor to use in an ongoing television currency panel, Nielsen commissioned a large enumeration survey of Hispanic households that began in 1991 and is still being conducted today. The sample frame for Nielsen's enumeration is composed of census block groups containing 95 percent of the Hispanic households in the U.S., which translates into about half of all block groups due to Hispanic density patterns. Slightly more than 39,000 random households are selected, which yields about 4,000 Hispanic completes (Los Angeles is slightly oversampled but represented proportionately in the national results). All homes are contacted using mail, phone, or an in-person visit. Mail is used primarily to screen out Non-Hispanic households. All Hispanic homes or any other type of home that does not respond to the mailing are either visited in person or by phone. This intense sampling regimen yields the following results in Los Angeles and for the remainder of the U.S.

Nielsen Enumeration Survey Results 2010

Status	Los Angeles		Rest of U.S.	
Complete interview	83.5%	100.0%	87.0%	100.0%
Basic	78.3	93.7	83.6	96.1
Alternate	5.3	6.3	3.4	3.9
No interview	7.6		4.2	
Non-household	8.9		8.8	
Cooperation rate	85.9		91.7	

With cooperation rates close to 90 percent, we have high confidence in the results produced. The core information gathered from this survey is the age, sex, and language use in home of each household member over age two. After collecting basic demographic data for household members, the respondent is asked which language each person speaks in the home. Four possible responses to this question are given: Only Spanish, Mostly Spanish, Mostly English, and Only English. Spanish/English Equally is accepted as a response if the respondent offers it. This personal language use is used to create a language value for the household as a whole based on the following matrix:

Only Spanish HHs	All persons must be Only Spanish speaking
Only English HHs	All persons most be Only English speaking
Mostly Spanish	Mixture of Only Spanish, Mostly Spanish, and Spanish/English equal speaking persons (or all Mostly Spanish)
Mostly English	Mixture of Only English, Mostly English, or Spanish/English Equal speaking persons (or all Mostly English)
Spanish / English equal	Homes containing both Spanish-Dominant (Only/Mostly Spanish) and English-Dominant (Only/Mostly English) persons

Based on the above classification system, household and personal language universe estimates are produced. The following are the Persons aged 2+ universe estimates for the current year based on both personal language spoken and household language classes:

Persons aged 2+ *by*	Household Language	Personal Language
Only Spanish	14.1%	25.8%
Mostly Spanish	28.0	26.6
Spanish / English equal	28.1	3.3
Mostly English	19.8	25.9
Only English	10.0	17.3

Note the differences between language in the home that is personally reported and the languages used overall in Hispanic homes. "Spanish/English equal" drops from 28 percent of the market on a household level to just 3 percent on a person's level. That is because very few people tell us that they speak Spanish and English exactly equally. Most folks tend to slightly more personal use of either one language or another. The source of most Spanish and English speaking homes is the ever-increasing tendency to have generational differences in language use present in the same home. Many of the Spanish and English equal homes are comprised of Spanish-dominant adults and English-dominant kids and teens while others contain English-dominant adults and Spanish-dominant seniors. As these types of household become more common, we have seen that Spanish and English equal households have been our fastest growing household segment:

The importance of the correct representation of the different language use groups both at the household and personal language level becomes apparent when we look at the different viewing levels by household language class for adults aged 18 to 49.

	All other tuning	English broadcast	English cable	Spanish broadcast	Spanish cable
Only Spanish	11.0%	4.8%	15.1%	59.1%	9.9%
Mostly Spanish	9.4	7.4	25.2	50.5	7.5
S / E equal	8.3	13.5	42.3	30.2	5.6
Mostly English	8.4	32.7	54.8	5.2	0.5
Only English	6.7	30.2	62.9	0.2	0.1

These dramatic divergences in viewing habits underline the importance of ensuring that each of these groups is represented properly in any sample and that post-stratification techniques used take language use or some other variable that takes the issue of acculturation into account.

Another point to consider when designing an Hispanic research effort is the optimum manner to contact the different language use (or other acculturation proxy) segments. Looking at the current installed Nielsen National Hispanic Sample, we see some fairly significant swings by the five language use groups for internet penetration, calling into question the ability of internet based studies to fairly represent all Hispanics.

Language Characteristics, Installed Sample

Percent of base with certain language characteristics that have computer or internet in the household.

	Computer	Internet
Only Spanish	34.2%	26.9%
Mostly Spanish	57.8	45.6
Spanish / English equal	72.5	61
Mostly English	80.4	71.9
Only English	87.3	83.1

Currently 26 percent of Nielsen's installed Hispanic sample does not have a listed land-line phone, compared with 18 percent of the total sample. While random digit dialing (RDD) can get around this somewhat, it appears that the old Hispanic marketing standby of listed Hispanic surnames is going to miss a significant portion of the population.

A few key takeaway points:

- There are real differences in media consumption behavior (at least) between Hispanic groups at different levels of acculturation. Nielsen's model has had great success for its purposes of measuring television viewing. While there are other possible ways of looking at this (some combination of census language proficiency and country of birth questions looks promising) any research study that does not find some way of taking acculturation into account runs a chance of significantly misrepresenting the market.

- While more and more research studies move to the internet for a variety of both research and business reasons, the low levels of penetration among Spanish-dominant Hispanics makes any purely internet-recruited study highly suspect as a tool for measuring Hispanics.

- Considering that over half of all Hispanics report that personally they speak more Spanish than English in their homes, you should be prepared to speak to them in the language they are probably speaking right before you contact them.

- The highest-quality study that I know of for the U.S. Hispanic market is Nielsen's enumeration study. The heart of that study is going to the door with culturally sensitive certified bilingual interviewers. Nielsen follows similar procedures in installing our people meter samples where, when matched against our enumerations, we do well in representing all levels of language use. Nielsen colleagues are using similar techniques in building their new Hispanic Homescan panel. This type of research is not always possible based on either financial or time constraints, but anything that is not directly reaching into Hispanic communities has to be measured against the yardstick of some research that does so, whether it is Nielsen Language Universe estimates or country of birth and language proficiency data from the Census Bureau's American Community Survey.

chapter 5

New Hispanic Market – New Media – New Strategies

Doing Hispanic Media the Right Way

Roberto Orci

CEO, Acento Advertising; President, Association of Hispanic Advertising Agencies (AHAA)

WITH the U.S. Census results front and center and the extraordinary growth the Hispanic market represents, marketing communications and media experts have been touting their version of the best approach to capitalize on the tremendous opportunity. You may even have heard starkly contrasting approaches:

The majority of Hispanics speak Spanish. And Spanish television reaches over 90 percent. With a one or two network buy, there's no need to go anywhere else.

The majority of Hispanics speak English. English television gets you the efficiency and the synergy of a "one voice" campaign.

In fact, each solution falls short for two reasons. The first is that to define an Hispanic simply by language use only is sophomoric. Segmentation has become much more helpful in determining how to effectively target your consumer. The second reason is that the Hispanic consumer is more complex than a passive single screen viewer that does not capitalize on engagement opportunities of non-traditional media.

Stay tuned. In the next few pages you will get the facts you need to know to assess a truly effective media plan aimed at Hispanics, as well as ensure you are getting the ROI you need from it. What may surprise you is that developing the most effective media plan is less about reach, frequency, and GRP (gross rating point) levels, and more about smart strategic decisions that are made at the outset. Smart media decisions are made in collaboration with multiple areas of an advertising agency, not just the hallowed halls of media planners and buyers.

Where Are You Going?

As you approach the Hispanic market as a growth segment for your business, defining your goals will be the most important first step. One reason is the likelihood that Hispanics may have a different relationship with your brand than your General Market segments. For instance, a Western Union wire transfer General Market customer sends money for emergencies or to children away at college in need of tuition or expense money. However, Hispanic customers will send money to family in their home countries regularly. In some cases they will wire money every two weeks. The obligation of supporting your family back home represents a much stronger emotional connection with a seemingly routine money transaction, and it makes sense that Western Union invests heavily to capture the money transfer Hispanic consumer segment. Understanding that can give more impact to your campaign plans.

Another example is an Hispanic smartphone user. She might not have a computer, but will use the phone for all her online needs, including entertainment. And the time she spends on the phone is more than a typical General Market customer so it stands to reason that the Hispanic customer will have a different relationship with her phone and her service provider.

#1 Rank in all mobile tasks and activities

	Non-Hispanic	Hispanic
Take photo	71%	79%
Text messaging	70	83
Send photo/video	52	61
Access internet	39	51
Email	34	43
Play game	31	40
Record video	30	42
Download App	28	36

	Non-Hispanic	Hispanic
Play music	27	47
Access social site	25	35
Watch video	21	39
Post photo/video	18	28
Online banking	15	25
Video call/chat	4	12

Source: Pew Research Center, 2011

In both the wire transfer and the smartphone cases, how you define your goals and how you envision growing Hispanic sales should be significantly different than your General Market plan. It boils down to differences in sources of volume that affect not only communication goals, but also media channel plans.

For example, are you targeting new users to the category, or will you go after leading brands' share in the category? Is your competitor in the Hispanic segment different than your General Market competitor? It might be.

A savvy marketer will do a side-by-side comparison of key consumer data in order to arrive at goals that will drive growth. That comparison will include not only awareness, but also differences in user demographics, competitive set, usage habits and attitudes, as well as qualitative research to understand how the product fits into a consumer's life. In the case of the money transfer category, we found that there was a lot of emotion attached to this transaction because the money usually went to a wife or parents back home who relied on the sender's support. Not so for the General Market user who uses it for the occasional emergency.

Who's Your Target?

"Hispanic women" is not a target definition, any more than something as broad as "Caucasian women" is. Surprisingly, your current Hispanic user may also not be your target. Here is an example to illustrate. When Honda first started advertising to Hispanics, its customer base was affluent, bilingual, educated Hispanic adults with one or two children—much like Honda's General Market customer. Honda could have concluded that all it needed to do was simply mirror its General Market creative campaign and media plans to reinforce its position. Honda also could have concluded that lower-income Hispanics were not potential customers. At the time, some even wondered if the Spanish-speaking segment could afford a pricey Honda Accord. In fact, most Hispanics had not considered a Honda because no one had ever invited them to drive one. And when Honda did issue the invitation, Accord and Civic quickly became the top two cars sold among Hispanics.

Here is where having Hispanic segment expertise available can help. You can quantify the opportunity by understanding who uses and who does not use your brand versus your competitors' brands. Importantly, this type of segmentation analysis is more about attitudes, beliefs and habits than it is about simple demographics. Despite having a lower household income than the General Market, Hispanics over index in many significant categories like food, clothing, cosmetics, and phone use, to name a few. This is more tied to cultural elements than it is to age and income. A qualified, well-informed marketer will know where to look.

Average annual expenditures
percent of disposable income, rounded to nearest whole number

	Hispanic	Non-Hispanic	Index for Hispanic
Housing	38%	34%	112
Food	15	13	113
Telephone services	3	2	132
Apparel & services	5	3	141
Transportation	17	15	110
Personal care	1	1	105

Source: U.S. Bureau of Labor Statistics Consumer Expenditure Survey, 2009

Here is a word of warning to those who assume that "acculturated" Hispanics are the ideal target. We hear this a lot because an acculturated Hispanic has been in the country longer, tends to have higher income, and be more familiar with U.S. brands. Therefore, it might stand to reason that you are better off using precious, scarce marketing dollars against this target. Here are two reasons why you might want to consider having a broader, expanded target.

The first reason to go after Spanish-dominant or unacculturated Hispanics is that they are in their early stages of adopting brands in the U.S. and, given their strong loyalty to brands and products that serve them well, you may be earning a customer for life. The second reason unacculturated Hispanics may be good business is that while they have lower incomes, they also have lower debt. This gives them the disposable income they can use to buy the brands they favor.

A Cautionary Word about "Acculturation"

You may have heard:

We want to target acculturated Hispanics.

Our General Market campaign already reaches acculturated Hispanics.

Spanish language advertising won't be needed when Hispanics become acculturated.

These are some of the common misperceptions about Spanish-language media and Spanish-language advertising, and they represent a fundamental misunderstanding of the acculturation process among American Hispanics. Language use and acculturation are not synonymous, and the process of acculturation is fluid.

Acculturation—the result of contact between two different cultures—is not a simple process like aging. In fact, with many variations, acculturation is multidimensional. Individuals engage in the process of acculturation in different ways depending on whether they are native- or foreign-born, their age, who they marry, their geographic location, their employment, and many other factors.

Language is just one of a number of dimensions on which Hispanics, and other ethnic groups, adapt to the prevailing U.S. culture. This spectrum includes food, entertainment, political engagement, leisure activities, fashion, and values. Focusing on the growing use of the English language by Hispanic Americans presumes that once an Hispanic learns English he is more like the General Market. That belief is mistaken.

Language preferred to speak by Hispanic adults, in percent

Only Spanish	25%
Mostly Spanish, some English	25
Mostly English, some Spanish	31
English only	19

Source: Experian Simmons NHCS 2010–2011

●　●　●　●　●

Multicultural research is full of examples of a sort of à-la-carte acculturation in which Hispanics are quickly and eagerly adopting some aspects of
mainstream American culture while holding on tightly to important aspects
of their Hispanic culture. Yankelovich MONITOR has found that 80 percent
of Hispanics agree that "Immigrants to this country should be prepared
to adapt to the American way of life," yet 87 percent also agree that they
"Feel need to preserve my own cultural traditions."

*Attitudes toward marketing and advertising among Hispanic adults,
2010–2011percent who agree*

	All Hispanic	Spanish-dominant	English-dominant
Spanish-language labeling on products helps me select what I want	38%	60%	17%
I remember more about or pay more attention to products/services that are advertised in Spanish	33	57	12
Spanish-language advertising is important to me because it's the best source of information for making purchasing decisions	30	51	10
When I hear a company advertise in Spanish, it makes me feel like they respect my heritage and want my business	42	27	29
I am much more loyal towards companies that show appreciation for our culture by advertising in Spanish	39	53	26

Source: Experian Simmons NHCS 2010–2011

Marketers such as Kraft ("What We've Learned About 'Acculturation,'"
viewpoint published in *MediaPost*) have found that understanding how
Hispanic consumers interact with their brands is the first step in capital-
izing on this growth opportunity.

A few illustrations of this dynamic in everyday life:

- Walmart stocks its Hispanic Supercenters with both dried beans in bulk and Welch's squeezable grape jelly, because Walmart has learned that Hispanic moms are shopping for family meals in which they value traditional foods and also shopping for their children who have acquired a taste for PB&J at school.

- According to The Associated Press-Univision Poll conducted in 2010 by the National Opinion Research Center (NORC) at the University of Chicago, 41 percent of Hispanic Americans observe *Semana Santa* (Holy Week, a religious holiday) while 75 percent celebrate the Fourth of July.

- Two of the most popular foods among Hispanic Americans are beans and rice **and** macaroni and cheese. One food comes from one culture and the other from their new adopted home.

- One in five Hispanic-American men watched both the Super Bowl **and** the World Cup tournament in 2010, again demonstrating that adopting some aspects of non-Hispanic American culture is not done at the expense of retaining an important part of Hispanic popular culture.

- Hispanics are as likely to eat peppers (54 percent) as they are to eat pickles (53 percent), and almost as likely to eat bagels (53 percent) as tortillas (66 percent). Go figure.

We also see examples of neo-acculturation, in which Hispanics experiment with some aspects of American culture, trying them on for size, so to speak, but then returning to their roots. Marriage and parenthood are often triggers, when Hispanic Americans re-assert the importance to the next generation of carrying on their language, values, cultures, and traditions.

●　●　●　●　●

Start with Creative that Reflects Culture

You can't have a discussion about media or channels without first ensuring that *what* goes on the air is as effective as *where* it appears. This oversight could cost you millions in media impact. An insightful marketer will ensure the General Market and Hispanic teams collaborate to seek out synergies where possible, and to ensure that the company or brand is represented consistently, even though the message might differ somewhat.

However, an astute executive will not insist that the Hispanic campaign mirror the General Market campaign. This is all too often the case because of the mistaken notion that having the same message across all media will result in increased effectiveness. Nothing could be farther from the truth. Numerous studies have shown that General Market and Hispanic Americans have different motivators as shown below.

Differences in motivators

	American	Latino
How we see ourselves	Individuals	A family
What we stress in relationships	Informality	Respect
What we instill in our children	Individuality	Respect for authority
On whom we reply for help	Institutions	Family & friends
How we regard our homes	An investment; "A point of departure"	"The Dream;" Sanctuary; a lifeline

Source: M. Isabel Valdés, Acento

Some categories appear more likely to take the easy way, to translate their English advertising and air it in Spanish. We see this often in retail, cosmetics, and movie advertising. We raise this communication issue in this chapter that covers media because it has a major impact on media effectiveness. Simply translating has the effect of cutting the impact of your media investment in half—that's millions of dollars in wasted spending.

The fact is that when you water down your Hispanic campaign in order to broadcast one message in the same exact way across segments, you diminish the effectiveness of the Hispanic program. Several studies, including one done by Roslow Research Group in 2006, have corroborated prior work on the subject by demonstrating that the English-language message is only half as effective, even among bilingual Hispanics, because it lacks cultural relevance. Studies have also shown that messages translated into Spanish are less effective than original advertising that reflects the target's culture effectively—sometimes referred to as *Transcreation*.

According to Roslow Research Group (2006), Spanish-language commercials are:

55 percent more effective at increasing ad awareness levels

50 percent more effective at message communication

4.4 times more persuasive

Now You Are Ready to Discuss What Language to Use

Some might see using Spanish or English as the result of having made an audience segmentation decision. They would be right. Others might see language choice as the result of a media plan decision to broaden Hispanic reach. They would also be right.

Except for the highly assimilated Hispanics who use English only, or the very Spanish-dependent Hispanics who use largely Spanish media, the majority of Hispanics use media in both languages. We have already seen smart marketers like Wells Fargo, McDonald's, and others use both Spanish and English language media effectively to target Hispanics. Their success is based on using English-language ads in a way that also appeals to General Market consumers. We now have at our disposal research tools that will help us quantify the appeal of this crossover advertising to multiple segments.

Language in which media is consumed
percent consumer media type of language among Hispanic adults age 18+

	Spanish only	Both	English only
Any	11%	75%	14%
TV	16	66	18
Radio	26	45	29
Magazines	27	29	44
Newspapers	25	22	52
Internet	10	33	57

Source: Synovate 2010 U.S. Diversity Markets Report

In the interest of marketing to a high-value and growing segment, reaching them in two languages makes sense. In our experience the main reasons not to fire with both language barrels have been budgets, or the difficult issue of which advertising agency to use—Hispanic or General Market. However, since we advocate aggressively courting fast growing segments like Hispanics, it is an issue worth considering. We also recommend measuring the results of all programs, Spanish or English, so you can make course-correction decisions based on quantifiable facts. This will allow you to charge ahead with confidence.

Recognize the Importance of Reach vs. Frequency

Marketers struggle with "how much is enough?" as well as "can I afford to go X markets deep on my budget?" Here is a solid tool to help you decide how to put together the right spending level for each market.

In many cases television and radio will absorb a large share of the media spend. The key here is to avoid going past the point of diminishing returns for every additional Reach Point. The chart below shows how you can predict the optimum weekly TV and radio weights using one of the many analytical media systems. After that point, you are better off integrating an additional media channel or stretching out the duration of your campaign. Of course, in the case of a direct-marketing campaign you may choose to increase your weekly frequency in order to bombard a narrowly defined audience in a short period of time. The charts below show the optimum TRP (target rating points) levels of the sample TV, radio, and combined TV plus radio plans.

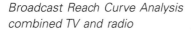

Broadcast Reach Curve Analysis
combined TV and radio

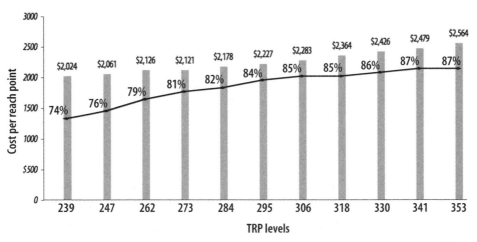

Another way to ensure you are not over-delivering media weight to the Hispanic audience is to follow the example below of estimating how many General Market TRPs are reaching Hispanics and then adding Spanish language TRPs to meet your goal. In the example below, the goal is 150 TRPs and 24 of them come from the General Market buy. This is after discounting English-language media weight by population, language, and cultural relevance. The discounting of the English-language weight levels is necessary and practical. It would be a mistake to assume that because Hispanics were in the audience they understood the message, or that it was culturally relevant and, therefore, effective.

Market "X" television
General Market Delivery of Hispanics; effective Hispanic weekly GRPs = 150

General Market schedule (GRPs)	175
General market delivery of Hispanics	72
Less 35% of Spanish-preferrred	47
Less 50% for lack of cultural relevance	24
Adjusted General Market delivery of Hispanics	24
GRPs from Hispanic/Spanish media buy	126
Total General Market + Hispanic/Spanish buy GRPs	150

Develop a Media Strategy with a Strong Strategic Foundation

The right media strategy is as much a creative exercise as it is a technical one. Consider that the first decision you must make is *what is the role of each media channel?* Broadcast might play a key role in raising top-of-mind awareness. But beyond that, how do you engage your customer? For example, in targeting sports enthusiasts you might extend your message to non-traditional channels like mobile apps with sports news and scores. Perhaps there is a role for bus shelters to reach your potential customer close to a retail outlet. Or if the subject is one that inspires passionate discussion, then a blogger site might be what you need.

Each channel should fulfill a specific role in your media plan. Keep in mind that the narrower your target market definition, the more likely it is you will use direct marketing media and other non-traditional channels. For instance, a retail bank marketer might use broadcast to widely promote its checking and savings packages, but might use mobile or even door hangers to promote its money transfer service product to households likely to have dependents in other countries.

Start by taking a mental inventory of how your product fits into the consumer's life and assess the media channels your potential customer is likely to favor, plus the state of mind he or she is in while engaged. You may find tremendous value in complementing your broadcast plan with the right non-traditional media vehicles. We have used advertising on the tops of washing machines in laundromats close to targeted retail outlets. We have also used ads on lunch trucks to reach recent arrivals to this country. And, we have used text messages to mobile phone users to give them a chance to connect with our telephone operators to take advantage of a time-sensitive offer. You will only know to explore these vehicles that can intercept your potential customers if you clearly understand your target consumer as more than a demographic. Below are the more common media vehicles and how their roles vary.

Television	Reaches mostly mass markets, provides audio-visual demonstrations, delivers cost efficiency
Radio	Reaches selective audiences, increases message frequency, reaches mobile populations
Print	Communicates sense of immediacy, allows for local emphasis, allows high fidelity color ads/inserts, catalog value
Outdoor	Allows geographic flexibility, provides 24-hour exposure, can align with store locations
Online	Provides message details, interacts with user, highly targeted, can direct traffic to website
Mobile (SMS)	Delivers call to action message, engages with consumer, captures database for remarketing
Direct Mail	Delivers call to action message, allows message depth, size/format flexibility, offers vehicle

Extending Media Investments and Efforts to the Experiential Level

Personal, one-on-one consumer experiences with a product or brand solidify a brand's image and awareness beyond mere advertising, which ultimately drives sales. Interacting with a brand outside of a commercial sell dovetails with today's Latino consumers' desire to make smart, savvy decisions based on their own life experiences, coupled with recommendations from family and friends.

Whether referred to as "Added Value" or "Media Boost," these elements should be heavily negotiated with every dollar you place. They aren't "freebies." They are the result of strong, deep partnerships with media suppliers. The lineup of components can take the form of any combination of elements selectively negotiated to ensure they align with specific overall campaign objectives, reinforce brand personality, and extend messaging. Here's a sampling:

Medium	Elements
Television	Bonus spots, on-air interviews, product integration, sponsorship billboards, in-program crawls, event participation, website integration, retail programs, access to celebrity talent
Radio	Bonus spots, DJ liners, on-air interviews, sponsorship billboards, event/remote participation, website integration, direct mail efforts, access to celebrity talent
Outdoor	Bonus showings, overrides, production elements
Print	Bonus insertions, premium positions, advertorials,
Digital	Bonus impressions, content, promotions, research/data collection
PR/Publicity	Brand spokesperson interviews, PSA airings, "news" coverage of community events, integrated segments, press releases, custom content

You can well imagine how this fully integrated media or channel approach results in a 360-degree or "surround-sound" program. Using media at the experiential level facilitates the connection process and allows you to benefit from the equity of the media, which helps to drive loyalty for your brand. It is a proven way to get more bang from your media investment.

Measure, Measure, Measure

At the end of the day a marketing program will be judged by its effect on business. In simplest terms, *did sales go up?* Fortunately, there are many ways to keep a finger on the pulse of your business. The chart below lists some of the metrics split up by area. Brand Sales can assess how well you are doing versus year ago, last month, weekly, and so on. Market Data can indicate how well you are doing relative to the marketplace competition and Brand Health is a good predictor of how you can expect sales to do in the future.

Measurement elements

Brand sales	Market data	Brand health
Sales volume	Market share	Brand awareness
Sales dollars	Distribution	Brand preference
Customer count	Sales velocity	Likes and dislikes
Ticket average	Hispanic store panel	Attitudes and use
Cost-per-call		Satisfaction metrics
Cost-per-sale		Online traffic
Promotion redemption rate		Social media reputation

Last, a heads-up. Though huge advancements have been made by marketers, retailers, and researchers in tracking Hispanic sales and the results of marketing efforts, Hispanic-related data is often lacking or incomplete.

For example, in the CPG and retail grocery categories, the tracking of "Hispanic sales" or share-of-market by syndicated sources often does not include a controlled sample or does not include the crucial Independent grocers. Hence, we know that market data still tends to under-represent the reality of Hispanic marketing and advertising campaigns.

Further, in proprietary research, all too often we see Hispanic break-outs of data that are a subsample of the General Market research based on Hispanic surname. Unfortunately, despite best intentions, these samples are typically not representative because they do not take into account language preference, length of time in the U.S., media use, and other crucial factors since the methodology is not originally designed to obtain a representative Hispanic sample.

Finally, Dispelling Some Myths

Here are some common (wrong) reasons managers give for not allocating media dollars to an Hispanic program. Read them and arm yourself for the inevitable discussion.

Current and foreseeable tough immigration policies will stunt Hispanic population growth. Why even bother?

Hispanic market growth is being fueled by both U.S. births and immigration. A review of 2010 Census data shows that the increase of the U.S. Hispanic population is now highly driven by births rather than immigration, contrary to past patterns.

Today 34 percent of the population under age 18 is Latino, underscoring this segment's youth.

Ninety-one percent of those under age 18 are native born, and therefore, a significant indicator of the type of growth we can expect in the near future. Among the older segment 53 percent are foreign born.

So what are the implications? Younger Hispanics will become more influential in purchase decision-making for the household, as they will have more experience with U.S. products and services and the overall consumer landscape. They will naturally assert a new identity that marketers will need to understand in order to connect with their feelings and thoughts.

With so many Hispanics now born in the U.S. they will assimilate more quickly. I can just reach them with my General Market plan.

Unlike previous waves of immigrants, Hispanics are not assimilating. By acculturating, they are retaining deeply held elements of Latino culture, while adopting the best of American life. This is reinforced and solidified by four primary realities:

- The segment is already a critical mass redefining the American mainstream;
- There is considerable pride in being Hispanic. Parents pass on language, food, religion, values, and so forth to U.S. born children;
- There is growing number of Spanish-language media options, plus the growing number of English-language properties catering to Hispanics;
- It is relatively easy to stay connected with family in home countries despite distances.

Hispanics are only important in a handful of markets like Los Angeles, New York, and Miami. Hardly worth mounting a major effort, is it?

Though certainly the Hispanic populations of major DMAs like Los Angeles, New York, and Miami continue to grow and flourish, the 2010 Census clearly revealed that the Hispanic population is increasing across every single state of the Union.

The states with the largest percent growth in their Hispanic populations include nine where the Latino population more than doubled, including a swath in the southeast United States—Alabama, Arkansas, Kentucky, Mississippi, North Carolina, Tennessee and South Carolina. The Hispanic population also more than doubled in Maryland and South Dakota.

In fact, in six states, growth in the Hispanic population accounted for all of those states' population growth. If the Hispanic population had not grown, Illinois, Louisiana, Massachusetts, New Jersey, New York, and Rhode Island would not have seen any population growth. In Michigan, the state population declined over the decade but the Hispanic population grew.

States with the largest Hispanic population growth, in percent

State	Growth 2000–2010
South Carolina	148%
Alabama	145
Tennessee	134
Kentucky	122
Arkansas	114
North Carolina	111
Maryland	106
Mississippi	106
South Dakota	103
Delaware	96
Georgia	96
Virginia	92

Source: U.S. Census Bureau, Pew Hispanic Center

I barely have enough budget to meet my General Market goals. I cannot afford to splinter my budget and weaken my main thrust.

As we've pointed out, marketing to the Hispanic segment is solely a business decision—a decision based on the mere fact that as a sizeable and growing consumer group, regardless of language preference, Hispanics are in the market for your goods and services, plus they have the disposal income that will grow your sales. Bottom line, marketing investments should follow opportunity, not language. Consider the population growth and the superior lifetime value of an Hispanic customer shown below.

Population growth 2000–2010

Hispanic	43%
Non-Hispanic	–5%

Source: U.S. Census Bureau/American Community Survey 2010; Geoscape-American Marketplace DataStream™ Series

Lifetime value

Hispanic	$2.52 million
Non-Hispanic	$2.17 million

Source: Aggregate Spending on Food, Personal Care, Apparel, Home Furnishings, Transportation, Entertainment, "Other;" Selig Center for Economic Growth

In closing, the Hispanic consumer represents the greatest potential for sustained growth in the U.S. today. At the current rate of expansion, Hispanics will drive population growth and, in turn, consumption in America for the next generation and beyond. Reaching Hispanics effectively should be at the top of every marketer's to-do list.

Projected U.S. Hispanic Population, 2010–2050
in millions and percent of U.S. population

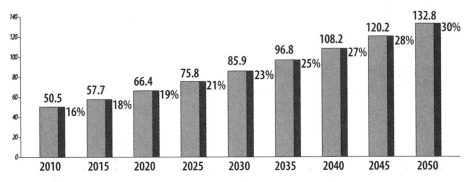

Source: U.S. Census Bureau ACS 2010, Geoscape-American Marketplace DataStream™ 2010 Series

The Hispanic Digital Market Opportunity

Lee Vann

CEO, Captura Group

THE U.S. Hispanic digital market continues to grow exponentially. Over 33 million Latino consumers can be reached via a computer or mobile device today. It has become a key and effective media that should be included in your Hispanic marketing campaigns, both national and or local. The critical mass is there and brands can cost effectively build relationships with these consumers to drive measurable objectives.

The Internet Market

As of September 2011, 33.3 million Hispanics were online, representing 66 percent of the total Hispanic population and 15 percent of the total U.S. online market. It is growing steadily and fast. Almost 5 million accessed the internet for the first time between September 2010 and August 2011 (comScore Media Metrix, 2011).

Online Hispanics are bilingual, using English and Spanish both in their daily and digital lives. Fifty-three percent online prefer to use the internet in English, 27 percent in both English and Spanish, while 20 percent prefer Spanish (comScore Media Metrix, 2011).

When compared with offline Hispanics, online Hispanics are younger, more affluent, and more acculturated, all characteristics that correlate with English-language preference. It must be noted however, that there is relatively little Spanish-language content online today, which often forces Hispanics, regardless of language preference, to consume digital content in English.

English-preferred online

English-preferred Hispanics behave similarly online to the General Market. They visit General Market websites, Facebook pages, and are exposed to General Market online advertising, blending easily and hence, are more challenging to reach with in-culture messages. Unfortunately, because of this blending into the General Market, some marketers draw the wrong conclusion, thinking that because their General Market online programs already reach English-preferred Hispanics, they don't have to do anything specific or in addition to cater effectively to this unique Hispanic market segment. However, we know from experience this is misguided. General Market marketing strategies and advertising messages will not resonate as strongly with these consumers because messages may not be on target or culturally relevant.

We know that the younger members of Hispanic households who tend to prefer English, are not only the trend setters among their peers, but also guide Spanish-preferred family members online, making them important message multipliers and influencers. As previously mentioned, English-preferred online Hispanics represent a large and attractive Hispanic online target segment, so it makes sense to engage with them in-culture and effectively. This means, even an English-language campaign should be conceptualized in-culture. Hispanic cultural cues can be infused into General Market campaigns by, for example, including Hispanic imagery, spokespeople, music, and language. The same approach applies to other multi-cultural market segments.

Marketers can use English language websites that cater to Hispanics such as Fox News Latino or use behavioral or interest-based targeting to reach them online in English. You can see why Hispanic advertising expertise is so valuable in a multi-cultural internet strategy.

Bilinguals online

Approximately 9 million or 27 percent of online Hispanics use the internet in both English and Spanish (comScore Media Metrix, 2011). This segment of the Hispanic online market moves fluidly between English and Spanish language websites. One minute they might be checking a bank balance online in English and the next catching up on news from their country of origin on a Spanish-language website. Marketers who want to reach them must do so in both English and Spanish, being mindful of the need for adding in-culture elements.

Spanish-preferred online

Twenty percent, or 6.5 million online Hispanics prefer and use the Spanish-language internet (comScore Media Metrix, 2011). Although the smallest of the three language segments, it is the fastest growing and the easiest to target. Because these users mostly consume online content in Spanish, marketers can easily engage them in standalone Spanish-language online programs that cater specifically to them. These Spanish-language programs can leverage myriad digital marketing tactics and can be easily measured because they can be isolated from general online marketing efforts. For marketers who want to reach the national U.S. online market, my recommendation is to develop distinct, yet complementary, English and Spanish-language online strategies.

The Hispanic Mobile Market

Mobile has emerged as a viable medium for reaching U.S. Hispanics. According to a 2010 Pew study, 76 percent of Hispanic adults were using cell phones in 2010. This is on par with African Americans (78 percent) but lower than Whites (85 percent). Similar to internet use, English-dominant Hispanics are more likely to use cell phones than Spanish-dominant Hispanics. The report indicates that 86 percent of English-dominant Hispanics, 78 percent of bilingual Hispanics, and 68 percent of Spanish-dominant Hispanics use cell phones.

Despite lower penetration rates, the same study found that Hispanics are active users of non-voice applications on mobile devices. Seventy-seven percent of Hispanic cell phone users access the internet, send or receive email, text message or instant message using their cell phones compared with 75 percent of Whites and 79 percent of African Americans.

A more recent study from the Florida State University Center for Hispanic Marketing Communication and DMS Insights found that English-preferred and Spanish-preferred Hispanics are more likely to have smartphones when compared with non-Hispanic Whites and African Americans. What's more, the study found that Spanish-preferring Hispanics are the ethnic group most likely to have an unlimited mobile data plan.

With the cost of smartphones and data plans continuing to decrease, I anticipate that use of these devices among Hispanics, including those that prefer Spanish, will increase dramatically. Many Hispanics will access the internet through a mobile device for the first time, leapfrogging traditional computer-based internet platforms. As a result, a sound Hispanic online strategy should consider mobile as a viable and growing medium to reach this segment.

Developing and Executing an Hispanic Digital Strategy

The rise of mobile and social media use has fundamentally shifted the way we think about communicating with Hispanics. In the past, a common approach was to translate a website from English to Spanish, refresh it every once in a while, and maybe drive traffic to it with online advertising. Today a more strategic and dynamic approach is necessary to successfully market to Hispanics via digital channels.

It is imperative to understand that marketing to Hispanics online is not easy or inexpensive. It requires a sound strategy, dedicated and specialized resources, a long-term vision, and adequate budgets. Your Hispanic digital strategy must begin with a clear research-based approach that delineates who you are trying to reach, what you are trying to accomplish, and how you are going to measure your success. Based on this strategy, we help our clients develop Hispanic digital communications platforms that are designed to reach the right audience, with the right message to drive key objectives in measurable ways.

As the name implies, an Hispanic digital communications platform is a set of processes and resources that are used to efficiently communicate with Hispanics via various digital channels. They can be as simple as one person engaging with Hispanics on Twitter to a large team building relationships with online Hispanics across multiple digital outlets. Marketers just getting into the Hispanic digital market might consider a phased approach. Develop a strategy that starts with a small platform and grow it based on predetermined milestones and goals.

Hispanic Digital Communications Platform

Hispanic digital marketing requires dedicated and specialized resources. Depending on the scope and complexity of the desired online program, a larger team with different expertise is recommended. However, the following are key to a successful program:

Executive Sponsor	An Hispanic digital marketing program must have executive level sponsorship to succeed. Such programs should not be afterthoughts or just translations of General Market programs. They should be a legitimate part of the overall marketing strategy and receive proportional budgets and resources. Today online Hispanics represent 15 percent of the U.S. online market, but marketers are spending a tiny fraction of their digital budgets on Hispanics.
Hispanic Digital Strategist	An Hispanic digital strategist is responsible for overall strategy and success of the program. This person must have extensive experience in both Hispanic and digital marketing and be constantly aware of the changes and trends occurring in both.
Hispanic Content Developer	Digital marketing is highly content driven. Supporting an Hispanic website, blog, Facebook page, or Google Adwords campaign requires skilled writers. In English or in Spanish, content developers communicating through digital channels must understand the culture and mindset of the target audience and have experience writing various forms of digital based content including, but not limited to, website content, blog posts, social media updates, banner copy, and text-based advertisements.
Hispanic Digital Designer	Bringing a communication platform to life requires a skilled designer who is in touch with the visual tastes of online Hispanics. If a program is being executed in Spanish, it is helpful for online designers to understand Spanish so they can efficiently create digital design elements that resonate with the target audience.
Hispanic Technologist	From content management systems to mobile applications, technology lies at the foundation of all digital communications. It is imperative for an Hispanic online marketing team to have a technologist that can bring creative ideas to life within a given technology infrastructure.

Hispanic Digital Communications Platform

Hispanic Digital Media Planner	The Hispanic digital media planner is responsible for executing digital advertising campaigns. Digital advertising is a complex discipline that consists of a multitude of tactics and technologies that are constantly changing. On top of that, reaching online Hispanics requires an additional layer of knowledge that makes a seasoned digital media planner critical.
Hispanic Digital Metrics Analyst	Digital communications platforms generate a fire hose of data that must be continuously analyzed. From website analytics and search engine optimization, to CRM and tracking the performance of online marketing campaigns, an Hispanic metrics analyst's job is to track campaign performance in near real time to drive optimization decisions and ensure that predetermined objectives are being met.

Hispanic Digital Marketing Tactics

When planning on using any Hispanic digital marketing tactic, marketers should be conscious of a few considerations up front.

First, it is critical to understand that Hispanic digital programs do not live in a vacuum. Organizations must consider how an Hispanic digital program will impact both internal operations and external touch points. From an internal perspective for example, it is important to consider how the digital program will be supported operationally including customer support, sales, returns, and even human resources. Hispanic digital programs should also be aligned with traditional marketing efforts so communications and messaging are complementary and consistent across channels.

Developing and supporting digital programs in Spanish adds a layer of complexity that marketers should be aware of and plan for up front. Perhaps most important, a skilled team of Spanish language content developers must be identified and included in the budget. In addition it is imperative to develop and document specific guidelines and processes that will govern the long-term development of Spanish-language content, including the tone of Spanish that will be used and the process for legal approval.

Hispanic website development

The cornerstone of most Hispanic digital strategies is a dedicated website. The most relevant insight I can share is that developing an Hispanic website requires the same effort, best practices, and resources as developing an equivalent General Market website. In addition, it is also important to understand and clearly define the relationship between the General Market and the Hispanic website.

Regardless of language preference, Hispanics toggle between English and Spanish websites, so there needs to be easy access between equivalent English and Spanish language websites. It is important that visitors to equivalent English and Spanish language websites perceive equal value from both. In many cases, the Spanish-language version of a website is significantly inferior to the English-language version leading Hispanics who compare the two to leave with a poor brand impression, and also hurting the company's reputation. To avoid this syndrome, the most important factor is planning and budgeting for long-term Hispanic website maintenance. The content, design, and technology on a website must be continuously refreshed in order for it to be successful. I have seen countless Spanish-language websites launch to much fanfare, only to see the English site evolve while the Spanish-language counterpart is neglected. When I see this happen I ask myself why launch a Spanish site in the first place.

Hispanic social media

In over a decade marketing to online Hispanics, I have never seen a more powerful, efficient and quantifiable medium for reaching Hispanics than social media. When I refer to social media, I am specifically referring to using popular social media platforms such as Facebook, YouTube, and Twitter to aggregate and engage with an audience. Hispanics have embraced these platforms in record numbers making social media a key tactic in any Hispanic digital marketing effort. The following table provides the total number of Hispanics that visited a given social network between August 2010 and August 2011.

Total number of Hispanic visitors to specific websites, in millions

	August 2010	August 2011	Growth, in percent
Hispanics Online	27.9	33.5	20%
Facebook.com	18.3	26.5	45
YouTube.com	16.3	24.3	49
Twitter.com	3.3	6.6	100

Source: comScore Media Metrix, 2011

Millions of Hispanics use social media today and they are among the most active users. High social connectivity is a part of Hispanic culture and more so among young Latinos. They need to stay connected to friends and families both inside and outside of the Unites States. They also need to share the cultural gap they experience today. Social media is the ideal vehicle for doing so.

Therefore, marketers must think beyond just driving traffic to an Hispanic website and instead think of social media as an extension of an online program. Social media sites such as Facebook, YouTube, and Twitter offer robust advertising platforms that make it easy and cost effective to aggregate qualified audiences of Hispanics. In addition, Hispanic response rates are higher. That said, the price of such advertising is increasing rapidly as more marketers use social media to reach Hispanics.

Hispanics are extremely open to engaging with brands that provide them with valuable and relevant content. By doing so, marketers can effectively build one-to-one relationships with online Hispanic consumers that can be leveraged to drive objectives in a measurable way. Hence, when an audience is aggregated, it is imperative to engage them with valuable, culturally relevant content on an on-going basis. Lastly, it is important to understand that the use of social media is not a silver bullet. It requires long-term investment in advertising to build an audience, and human resources to maintain and measure an active dialogue with this community.

Email marketing

Although not as sexy as other digital marketing channels, email remains one of the most effective, efficient, and measurable ways for reaching Hispanics online. In August 2011, 22.8 million or 68 percent of all online Hispanics used a web-based email service such as Yahoo! Mail, Hotmail, or Gmail (comScore Media Metrix, 2011). When it comes to email, the primary tactic recommended is an opt-in email program specifically geared to Hispanics. Opt-in email programs allow marketers to build a proprietary database of contacts that can be leveraged to communicate with efficiency and frequency. As discussed previously, there is limited availability of high-quality Hispanic content online and this is also true with email. As a result marketers can expect higher open rates and click through rates on high-quality Hispanic-focused, opt-in email programs than they would see with the General Market.

Hispanic Mobile Tactics

Although 76 percent of Hispanic adults own a cell phone and many actively use them for non-voice applications (Pew Hispanic Center, 2011), Hispanic mobile marketing is a new and fast moving discipline that must be considered strategically. The simplest way to reach Hispanics on their mobile devices is to use social media. Leading social media and blogging platforms provide mobile optimized version of their sites. If you have an Hispanic Facebook page you also have an Hispanic mobile presence.

Mobile tactics that require incremental resources and investment should be carefully weighed against the target audience and objectives of a given effort. These include developing a mobile version of an Hispanic website, creating native mobile applications, and mobile advertising. Of these tactics, creating a mobile friendly version of your Hispanic website is a logical first step. Mobile friendly websites are typically less costly to build and maintain when compared with native mobile applications. This is because a mobile friendly website will work across most mobile browsers, whereas native mobile applications must be customized for the constantly changing iPhone, Android, Blackberry platforms. Mobile advertising typically requires a mobile website or native application to drive traffic and can include display advertising on mobile websites or text-based advertising. Similar to opt-in email marketing, marketers can develop an opt-in text program to proactively communicate with Hispanics via text messaging.

Hispanic Online Advertising and Outreach

Each strategy outlined above requires a long-term investment in Hispanic online advertising and outreach to succeed. The following sections highlight the main online advertising and outreach tactics that are available to marketers and provide insights into what we have found successful.

Each month 29.2 million or 87.6 percent of online Hispanics visit a search site like Google, Yahoo! Search, or Bing. This massive audience combined with the ability to reach users as they search for specific products and services makes search engine marketing one of the most effective advertising methods for reaching Hispanics.

Search engine marketing consists of both search engine optimization (SEO) and paid search engine advertising. When compared with the General Market, search engine marketing to Hispanics is less competitive but there is also significantly less volume. The best practices of search engine optimization (SEO) should be implemented across an Hispanic digital communications platform in order to effectively reach Hispanics through search engines. Regarding paid search campaigns, we have found Spanish language keyword search volumes steadily increasing as more and more Hispanics come online. Although the cost per click for Spanish keywords has increased, it is still significantly lower than equivalent English keywords. Paid search engine marketing is typically thought of as a direct response strategy, but it can also be used to cost effectively build brands and awareness among Hispanics, by using banners on relevant websites offered by the content networks of the major search engines.

Facebook *Habla* In-culture!

Facebook has quickly become a powerful Hispanic digital advertising platform. It allows marketers to target audiences based on geographic, demographic, language, and psychographic characteristics. We have leveraged Facebook's targeting engine to reach various segments of the Hispanic online market by using some of following tactics: geographic targeting to reach DMAs and zip codes that have a high concentration of Hispanics; language targeting to home in on Spanish-preferring U.S. Hispanics;

and interest-based targeting to reach bilingual and English-preferring Hispanics.

Another digital advertising tactic is to work with Hispanic-focused publishers and advertising networks such as Univision.com and MSN Latino. They allow marketers to purchase targeted banners on a cost per thousand basis and also to negotiate custom sponsorships and promotions. Hispanic advertising networks and exchanges aggregate a large number of Hispanic websites and users and allow for broader reach, and better targeting typically at a lower cost compared with Hispanic publishers. Click through rates on banner campaigns aimed at Hispanics tend to be higher than click through rates on equivalent General Market campaigns. This table summarizes the top publishers and networks in terms of Hispanic online reach according to ComScore.

Top publishers and networks for Hispanics online, in millions

	August 2011	Hispanic Reach
Hispanic Online Market	33.5	100%
Pulpo Media	13.3	40
Batanga Network	6.9	21
Orange Network	4.6	14
EZ Target Media	4.3	13
Univision Communications	3.3	10
Yahoo! Network Plus Hispanic	2.7	8
Terra	2.0	6
Audience Science Hispanic Channel	2.0	6
Hola Networks	1.8	5
MSN Latino	1.7	5

Source: ComScore, 2011

Two Examples

GobiernoUSA.gov

GobiernoUSA.gov is the official Spanish language portal of the U.S. government. Its mission is to provide timely and relevant official U.S. Government information in Spanish. To accomplish this objective,

GobiernoUSA.gov has developed a multi-faceted Hispanic communications platform to engage with Spanish speakers online and serve as the official directory of the U.S. government in Spanish. With approximately 500,000 visitors per month, GobiernoUSA.gov is optimized for mobile users and also features original, culturally relevant Spanish language articles and videos. GobiernoUSA.gov proactively reaches out to Spanish speakers online by distributing content to Spanish language websites, communicating through an opt-in email program, and proactively using social media such as Facebook, Twitter, and YouTube.

Vivemejor®

Unilever's Vivemejor is a cross-category, multi-brand initiative engaging Hispanic women during their most important consideration moments—online as they gather information and in-store at the point of purchase. Vivemejor has successfully tapped into the Hispanic digital market by creating a platform that drives business objectives. It consists of a dedicated Spanish language website, www.vivemejor.com, that supports Unilever personal care and food brands through original, culturally relevant Spanish language content. The site also features a mobile optimized version and a targeted opt-in email program. The Vivemejor platform also consists of a vibrant Facebook community, www.facebook.com/vivemejor, of approximately 100,000 Latinas. The entire Vivemejor platform is supported by a robust Hispanic online advertising strategy.

Captura Group enables leading companies to harness the power of online channels to deliver a compelling experience that provides user value and accomplishes business objectives. From strategy development to online program execution, in English or in Spanish, our work spans across different cultures but has one thing in common: measurable results that make a difference to your business and to your customers. *www.capturagroup.com*

Building Deep Connections with Latinas

Lucia Ballas-Traynor,
Co-founder and EVP, CafeMom

BEYOND the size and fast paced growth of the Latina population segment in the U.S., what makes them an especially attractive target is not only the fact they "hold the purse string" power of a large share of the trillion dollar disposable income of the Hispanic market today, but also their unique socio-demographic characteristics, Hispanic households are larger, and due to Hispanic cultural characteristics, chances are they will continue to have larger households for a longer time than other cultural segments! Over half a million new Latino homes are created every twelve months. Latinas are on average much younger than the General Market of women, fueling most of the population growth in the nation. Furthermore, today's Latinas wield unprecedented levels of influence in every aspect of American society as they attain greater levels of education, economic power, political and cultural clout. As a vital and growing demographic force in the marketplace, they are a highly desirable segment to sell to and become friends with. More acculturated Latinas are growing the numbers of Latina-owned businesses and they are more likely to enter professional occupations than previous, immigrant generations—even more so than Hispanic males.

Working from the basic demographics of this segment is just the first step; you need to establish a meaningful connection with these powerful women shoppers.

As the numbers in the table below illustrate, this is the consumer segment that you must target, as it will shape the brand preferences and tastes preferences of a large segment of the American marketplace. Based on the 2010 Census and popula-tion growth projections, we know that over 50 percent of the total U.S. population is going to be multi-cultural just 30 years from now. Many of these American Latinos are already born, and will live in a Latino household!

U.S. Latinas by the numbers

Number of U.S. Latinas	24 million
percent of total Hispanic population	51%
percent of total U.S. female population	16%
percent born in U.S.	48%
percent born in Latin American countries	52%
percent of those born in Mexico	60%
median age of Latinas	27 years
median age of Non-Latinas	41 years
median age of U.S. born Latinas	18 years
number of U.S. born Latinas	15 million

Note: Does not include Puerto Rico. Sources: U.S. Census Bureau, Pew Research Center

The Mom and Acculturation Factors

- Over 21 percent of all mothers in the U.S. with children aged 2 to 11 are Hispanic.

- 26 percent of Latinas are mothers by age 19, (versus 22 percent African American and 11 percent Whites).

- One in four babies born in the U.S. are Hispanic.

- 55 percent of *all* Hispanic women report they speak only English in their home while 73 percent of Foreign-born Latinas do not speak English in their home.

- Latinas have completed less schooling than non-Hispanic women; over one-third have less than a high school degree, compared with 10 percent of non-Hispanic White women.

- Labor force participation rate is similar among Latinas (59 percent) and non-Hispanic women (61 percent), but most Latinas are in administrative and office jobs.

Cultural Passion Points that Work!

To drive brand favorability, purchase intent, and to generate exponential consumption among Latinas, it is important to understand and leverage the cultural passion points that define and differentiate them.

All women who classify themselves as Hispanic or Latina—regardless of where they were born, how many years they have lived in this country, and whether they use Spanish or English more regularly—share a common and unifying cultural heritage and value system.

There is an extensive body of literature that talks about Hispanic cultural traits and this is not the place to dive deeply into these. However, these cultural traits can be used in the digital social marketplace.

Latinas' Highly Social Behavior Extends into Digital

Hispanics are highly social. Most aspects of their lives revolve around social or group activities. And we see this reflected in the "digital society." More than 30 million total Hispanics are estimated to be online in the U.S. and their presence is growing at two times the pace of the rest of the General Market internet population. Hispanics also rank among the highest users of mobile devices over-indexing in text messaging and time spent interacting on mobile phones or accessing social media networks.

Even less acculturated Latinas have moved beyond basic internet use to connect with friends and family abroad and as a primary source of information. Now we find them deeply engaged in the use of socialization tools. They are joining social media networks to connect and share information with other like-minded Latinas who share their interests. They are downloading, creating, and sharing music and videos; they are posting *abuela*'s recipes adapted to modern day, photos of family trips, and a growing number of *blogueras* are connecting and empowering Latinas across the country with tips and advice on living

Latin Beauty is at the Core of Every Hispanic Woman's Identity

For most Latinas, looking (and smelling) good is an everyday priority. To look good means to feel good about every aspect of who they are. For Latinas, the bare essentials are not enough. As a group, Latinas spend significantly more on beauty and apparel than non-Latinas. Most Hispanic research shows that the Latin notion of beauty dominates across all levels of acculturation. Among the less acculturated, beauty ideals are deeply rooted in Latin culture "looks." As Latinas acculturate, the Latin and American beauty ideals are fused and consequently, the Latin beauty standards are somewhat more flexible and relaxed.

People En Español's 2009 HOT Study: "What Matters Most to Women During Recessionary Times," demonstrated that despite the difficult economy and the impact it had on Latinas' disposable income, beauty product consumption stayed close to pre-recession levels. Grocery was the only other category where consumption levels were maintained. The study showed that Latinas were making tradeoffs, like giving up their Frappuccinos, in order to buy their favorite lipstick or perfume.

The internet provides marketers and content providers the opportunity to personalize the beauty experience for Latinas. For example, makeover tools like the highly-trafficked "Cambia Tu Look" makeover tool in *peopleenespanol.com* provides Latinas with the opportunity to try on the looks and trends they've been spotting but with hair colors, eye color, and photos featuring the shapes and shades that truly represent real Hispanic women. The interactive makeover tools can feature the looks of top Latin telenovela stars like Jacqueline Bracamontes, teen idols like Anahi and Belinda from Hispanic TV, as well as top American Hollywood celebrities.

Bicultural Reality Unites Latinas

The single most unifying and defining cultural characteristic that distinguishes U.S. Hispanic women regardless of nativity and language usage from both their Anglo and Latin American counterparts is their bicultural identity and reality. Latinas are constantly "modulating" two cultures and value systems that at times come in direct conflict. They are learning to adjust their cultural temperature up or down depending on the roles that they are playing, the circumstances that they are living, and the environment that surrounds them.

Latino Roots Dominate in More Traditional Roles

At home, Latino roots and value systems dominate, regardless of acculturation. For example, in-culture imagery shows Latinas as caregivers, caring for an elderly parent at home rather than placing him or her in a facility. Similarly, in a medical or hospital related advertisement, you might show a Latina accompanying her parents to the doctor and acting as a facilitator and translator, rather than sending them off on their own. Like other mainstream women, today's Latinas are juggling it all. But *unlike* Anglo women, who have a history of balancing work and life, Latinas are new at it and they also have to deal with the need to modulate and strike a balance between two distinct cultures and value systems.

Not an easy task! The traditional role of mom is undergoing transformative change. The majority of Latinas are raising U.S. born, "American" children, juggling increased responsibilities and continuing to learn how to navigate and crack the

American code while still trying to hold on to the Hispanic social behavior that makes them uniquely Latina.

Examples abound as leading marketers use empowerment platforms that also validate and celebrate Latinas' bicultural reality as a way to connect them, to gain their loyalty, induce trial, and generate results. For example, during the recession one detergent brand sponsored workshops for Spanish-speaking Latinas on financial literacy and managing household finances. Kmart's "Madres y Comadres" and "Latina Smart" platforms are among the best and most current examples of a company that has leveraged key and unique insights on Latinas to drive their messaging and brand engagement and favorability.

A SOCIAL PLATFORM CASE STUDY

Use Social Media to Deepen Connections with the Evolving Latina Mindset

Just as in the General Market, in the Hispanic digital landscape it is the general interest portals like Yahoo, AOL, and Univision as well as huge social media networks like Facebook and YouTube that dominate. But these big players do not fulfill the unique needs and interest of the Hispanic segments. This is why you will see a proliferation of content sites that are vertically programmed like *peopleenespanol.com* that targets the celebrity-obsessed audience, *todobebe.com* for Spanish speaking moms and others, or online communities that revolve around shared interest or topics that are very specific.

I am currently working for CafeMom—the number one website in the country for moms— as co-founder and EVP, leading the development of a new site that will be dedicated to serving the interests and needs of Latina moms. The name of the site, "Mamás Latinas" came from the community and was selected from a list of many other names. This demonstrates how the Latina community will fuel everything we do. To satisfy this need, we are creating an electronic, social meeting place that will allow Latinas to connect with other likeminded women. Unlike other platforms, the conversations taking place in the Mamás Latinas community will power the content that we curate and generate from regular moms, celebrities, experts and bloggers who understand and embody the unique needs, interests, and experiences of Latina women.

Recently we launched a Soy Mama Latina Facebook fan page. We are finding that although there are fewer Spanish-dominant Latinas online, they are much more engaged than their English-dominant counterparts. They write long entries when they post. They are willing to provide information beyond what we ask. Followers of a similar page in English are less engaged around similar topics. In short, Spanish-dominant Latinas are hungry to connect with others like them and hungry for information in their own language and they are responsive to brands and companies that make the effort to talk with them.

The Latina moms—U.S. born, bilingual, or English-dominant—are much more integrated into American society, but still look for guidance in some areas and use the internet and social tools to seek resources that allow them to succeed in America and maintain their culture and their Spanish-language. These are key elements to raising successful, socially adapted, and integrated children in mainstream American society. They want to engage in conversations with other Latinas who understand what matters to them most—their unique life priorities and passions.

Our mission is to build a web destination that engages and empowers Latina moms across the U.S. by providing them with a bilingual site where they can connect with millions of other Latina moms around common interests, needs, and lifestyles.

A Look Ahead

Latinas are fueling and shaping the future of this great country. It is crucial that media, marketers, business and political leaders find ways to learn, to succeed and empower this segment to operate in an increasingly complex world. How can Latinas aspire to succeed if the only faces and experiences they see are the ones reflecting the lives of the mainstream? Our online dialogue with "mamás Latinas" shows that key and traditional Hispanic cultural insights are still there and strong particularly with the Latina Mama. However, these cultural insights are evolving as they acculturate and social media platforms can be great places to meet them, promote your brands and services, and build long-term emotional connections.

Mamás Latinas, part of **CafeMom,** launched in January 2012. Mamás Latinas is poised to become the leading, trusted bilingual online destination dedicated to connecting, informing, entertaining, and empowering Latina moms by serving their unique cultural interests and needs. CafeMom is the number one site on the internet for moms and the premier strategic marketing partner to brands that want to reach moms in the digital environment. Lead investors are Highland Capital Partners and Draper Fisher Jurvetson. CafeMom was founded by Andrew Shue and Michael Sanchez. *www.cafemom.com*

Leveraging Hispanic Newspaper Platforms to Build Your ROI

Martha Montoya

Co-owner, El Mundo Newspaper; President, Los Kitos Entertainment, Los Kitos Produce; Board member, USHCHC; VP Membership, NAHP

Five reasons why Hispanic print is thriving

Hispanic newspapers offer a path to build ROI by combining advertising, supplier diversity, community outreach and sustainability into an integrated approach towards the growing Hispanic market. They remain a healthy vital part of the Hispanic communities they serve and they understand that readers are changing their media consumption patterns over time. Hispanic newspaper publishers expect to evolve with their readers by launching appropriate new media forms with content relevant to their communities. As a group Latinos are younger, but according to studies by the Pew Hispanic Research Center, they are still less likely to access the internet, have a home broadband connection, or own a cell phone than Whites are. This limited access to other media gives newspapers voice and place in their communities.

Here are five reasons why you should consider newspapers as an important medium for reaching Hispanics.

One: Hispanic readers are younger than readers of Anglo daily newspapers

Hispanic readers are young! 57 percent are age 34 or younger (*Hispanic Readership Study*, Readership Institute, *www.readership.org*).

Two: Hispanics are highly engaged with their newspapers

Hispanic newspapers enjoy an 86 percent readership compared with 48 percent readership of Anglo daily newspapers. (Center for Hispanic Marketing Communications)

Hispanics are also regular readers and spend a significant amount of time with their Hispanic newspaper of choice (*Editor and Publisher*).

Hispanic publications have 3.5 readers per copy and 83 percent have responded to an advertisement (*2008–2010 U.S. Diversity Markets Report,* Synovate).

Three: Hispanic print has not slowed down contrary to mainstream

English-language dailies saw a 5 percent decline for the six-month period from March to September 2010 versus Hispanic daily papers, which grew circulation by 1.9 percent (Pew Research Center's Project for Excellence in Journalism; *State of the News Media: An Annual Report on American Journalism 2011*).

The total number of Hispanic newspapers remained stable in 2010 (832 versus 835 in 2009), according to the Latino Print Network. And the largest cohort—weekly publications—grew by 18 percent to 117 papers.

Four: Hispanic newspapers play a unique role as a community conduit

Hispanic newspapers readership strength is rooted in its unique role as a community conduit, focusing on the news, the needs, and the aspirations of the Hispanic community. Their unique relationship with their readers provides exclusive local content, while acting as the primary funnel to engage the community. Advertisers benefit from deep reader involvement, building grass roots support for their products and services.

Five: Content, content, content

Cultural relevance connects while language and content are the connectors that will stay regardless of the vehicle.

Los Kitos Produce (farms, packing house and fruit grower/operator), Los Kitos Entertainment (a syndicated cartoon strip/content provider) and *El Mundo Newspaper* (largest and oldest Hispanic newspaper in Washington State), are all owned, in part, by Martha Montoya who is leading several initiatives on a local and national level to advance the position of minority-owned businesses. *www.loskitos.com*

The Art that Needs to Change

Federico Subervi, Ph.D.
Professor and Director of the Center for the Study of Latino Media and Markets
School of Journalism & Mass Communication, Texas State University-San Marcos

M. Isabel Valdés, M.A.,
President, IVC In-Culture Marketing, San Francisco, California

THE marketing research industry has re-invented itself over the past two decades through the use of online and computer-based consumer interviewing and data-gathering technologies, bringing benefits such as increased efficiency, lower costs, and faster turnaround to market researchers and data users alike.

However, some Hispanic marketing and research experts have raised concerns that the pervasive use of computer-based and online consumer research are not adequate to study the Latino market, since a significant number of Hispanic consumers do not have access to a personal computer or laptop. Other Latinos overlooked are those who have access to a computer and navigate the web, but are not reached or are not comfortable participating in online studies.

These are segments of the Latino market that are "high-value" for many industries that count on them for their ongoing business growth plans. They require accurate, reliable market data with insights about the unique needs, wants, and best marketing approach for both bilingual Latino customers and low-to-no English Latinos. Estimates are that Hispanic marketing studies conducted mostly or only online, or just with the

English-speaking Latino consumer segments can exclude from 30 to 50 percent or more of the U.S. Hispanic market depending on the business category studied.

The lack of reliable marketing data from all Hispanic consumers makes it difficult to successfully estimate the true size of the business opportunity and marketing insights to target the total Latino market as noted by several experts in this book. Therefore, this is a huge issue that needs to be addressed with industry input.

Goals and objectives

Findings from a recent study funded by HACR, together with the insights provided by corporate executives interviewed in the second phase of the study, provide guidelines to improve the quality and reliability of marketing research data made available to corporate America and other Hispanic consumer data users.

The HACR study tries to answer the following questions:

1. What are the research methods most commonly recommended and used by established primary marketing research companies to conduct national Hispanic marketing research studies for Fortune 500 and 1000 companies (e.g., online, telephone, door-to-door, CADI, mail, intercepts, or a combination of the above)?

2. What socio-cultural and economic variables are included?

3. Which specific sample sizes, markets or cities are more commonly recommended to be included in a national marketing research study?

4. How reliable and projectable are the recommended methodologies to study and track the "entire" Hispanic consumer market?

The Study

The assessment consisted of an online survey, followed by a phone interview.

Of 99 firms identified as doing Hispanic market research, 31 met the criteria established for the study. They conducted original primary research with Hispanic consumers, had offices in the U.S., had national full service research capabilities, had experience in market research on consumer packaged goods, and were established prior to 2006.

The methodology

A standardized "case study" was developed which presented a hypothetical consumer packaged goods (CPG) client *"planning to target the total U.S. Hispanic market—separately from the General Market—for the first time."* Based on this case study, survey participants were asked to make recommendations by responding to 10 questions. The questionnaire was fielded online. Only 15 out of 31 companies provided sufficient completed information to be used for the analysis. Therefore, the results of this study cannot be generalized to the total Hispanic marketing research industry. However, we are confident that the findings provide valuable, directional insights.

Findings

The sample size

After presenting the hypothetical case, participants were asked, *"What sample size would you recommend for a first, national entry level study?"* Recommendations ranged from 300 to 3,000. The most frequently recommended sample size was 1,000 participants.

Without getting into the technicalities of research methodology, the sample size is a very important feature in any empirical study whose goal is to make inferences—or projections—about a population from a sample. This determines the statistical power, that is, the predictability, reliability and credibility of the results. A small sample size lacks the statistical power, hence, the credibility to represent the population studied, and the data gathered may lead to wrong assumptions and decision-making.

To size the business opportunity towards a national market entry investment based on a small, non-projectable or non-representative national survey study, such as a 300 person study sample recommended by some research companies, and base multi-million dollar decisions on directional or qualitative research data only, such as use of focus groups alone, can lead to major failures in market value assessment and expected return on investment (ROI). This may lead to poor business planning and poor results. Management may then erroneously conclude, "There is no business opportunity with the Hispanic market." Sadly, this tends to be a common practice in Hispanic marketing with the consequent disappointing ROI and withdrawal of Hispanic businesses from the marketplace.

Corporations targeting a $1.3 trillion-market segment such as the U.S. Hispanic market—54 million people when Puerto Rico is included— should allocate robust marketing research budgets and also demand from their Hispanic marketing research vendors the same professional and high standards requested for General Market data, intelligence and consumer studies.

The interviewing method

Higher consistency was observed in response to the question: *"Which method(s) would you recommend?"* All companies, except for two, recommended using individual interviews for survey studies and several recommended a mix of research methods, such as survey interviews together with qualitative research methods. Qualitative consumer learning deepens the data gathered in typical survey interviews, which tend to be brief and do not allow for in-depth probing on a variety of topics. Focus groups add unique value and insights to a successful business and marketing communications strategy that cannot be obtained in any other way.

Interviewing method

Options provided to interview consumers included telephone interviews, online surveys, in-person intercepts, mail surveys, door-to-door surveys, or some other method. Most said they would use the telephone in combination with other data-gathering methods including the internet studies and intercepts, (personal interviews conducted randomly in public places, such as malls, stores, parking lots, etc.). Only two companies offered a method that would ensure obtaining responses from Hispanic consumers who might be unavailable with phone and internet technologies. One company would gather information with Hispanic consumers using exclusively door-to-door interviews, the method that is most certain to reach out to the full spectrum of subjects, the second company a mix of telephone and door-to-door survey interviews. The right mix and reliability of the different interviewing methods is a complex research subject and beyond the scope of this book. However, several contributors in this book address these concerns and propose recommendations. (See chapters by César Melgoza, Carlos Garcia, and Doug Darfield.)

Length of interview

"If conducting individual interviews, what is the length of interviewing time (recommended) with each respondent?" Research companies recommended from as little as 15 minutes to as long as half an hour. The latter is the recommended option.

Given the many cultural nuances and complexities of the Hispanic market, including the fact that it takes approximately 10 to 15 percent more time to communicate similar information in Spanish vis-à-vis in English, the longer the interviewing time, the better the chances of obtaining the minimal data needed as well as deeper cultural insights. Again, it makes little business sense to invest millions of dollars in new product development or in the development of a national marketing communications campaign, for example, and attempt to save money on primary marketing research data that would lead to the development of a successful business strategy.

Yes, this can be costly and can pose operational challenges and sometimes, delays. Nevertheless, a well-designed marketing research study is a must, and should be viewed as an investment, the first line item in the budget of a corporation aware of the "true value" and potential of the growing U.S. Hispanic market.

Market selection

The question: *"What DMAs/Markets would you utilize?"* allowed respondents to list up to ten Hispanic market options. The four largest Hispanic markets were mentioned by all respondents: Los Angeles, Miami, New York and Chicago; fourteen also added Houston to this mix.

The selection of the regions, markets or cities where a study will be conducted is highly relevant as can be expected with such a diverse market segment as the U.S. Hispanic market. Even though the majority of the market is of Mexican origin or decent, the context can vary greatly, that is, the cities where they reside are unique as markets and the dynamics even within the Mexican-heritage segment may differ. For example, the shopping behavior of a Mexican-heritage consumer in downtown Los Angeles can vary greatly from that of a Mexican-heritage consumer in San Antonio or Chicago. In addition, it is well known that the U.S. Hispanic market is culturally diverse (i.e., the Latino population comprises people with Mexican, Caribbean, Central and South American heritage) and that each city or market (e.g., Los Angles, Miami, New York, Chicago, San Jose) can vary significantly in the number of residents from those diverse cultural backgrounds. Thus, it is highly valuable to have a comprehensive picture of the differences and similarities of the *national* Hispanic market to devise well-tuned marketing, retailing, and communications efforts.

It is possible to talk *national* Hispanic marketing once the local differences and similarities are well known and clear to the decision-makers. A comprehensive body of knowledge on a per market basis also helps marketing managers contemplate the choice to target each Hispanic market or region separately, rather than as one national market. In some instances, it may be more effective "to talk local," in the unique local Latino consumer culture rather than to spend advertising dollars on a national campaign that is not culturally in-tune with the local Latino consumer. Last, Hispanic market targeting options can vary drastically by business category and strategy. These decisions can be made if local know-how and data are available for consideration in the decision-making grid and diagnostics.

Definition of a "national Hispanic sample"

For some, the "national Hispanic market" should include the entire territory of the U.S., regardless of the number of Latinos residing in some areas. The end result is that data would be gathered from towns or cities with a very small number of Hispanic consumers or households where consequently no Hispanic marketing efforts exist, nor will exist because it makes no business sense. The data from these studies can "muddle" the real picture in the marketplace and under-represent the opportunity or the results of a marketing effort, as data from areas targeted with Hispanic retailing or advertising and those not targeted are mixed up in the same bowl. Other corporations approach the Hispanic market on a regional basis, because this fits the blueprint of their sales organizations. Again, if Hispanic consumers are interviewed in cities or towns where no Hispanic marketing programs take place, the results will misrepresent or under-represent the true results and impact of the regional Hispanic marketing efforts.

The present study suggests that there is agreement among Hispanic marketing research companies regarding the definition of a National Hispanic Sample. Since the Hispanic market concentrates largely in a few states, focusing on these would include in the study sample at least 80 percent of the total national Hispanic population. Six companies recommended nine or 10 cities, which would provide a comprehensive and rich baseline of data, and the remaining companies would include between five to seven cities, also a good national Hispanic market sample. Usually the same markets as stated earlier.

This is good news. However, this may not be the right approach in some cases. Some products or services may be more attractive to Mexican border Latinos, and not to others, or some emerging non-Hispanic traditional Hispanic markets may present a more interesting consumer target for specific products and services. Hence, the final selection of states or cities to include in a study should vary accordingly. Hispanic research companies should be aware of these differences and make recommendations to clients accordingly.

Socio-demographics and acculturation

Conducting consumer studies of Latinos requires consideration not only of the basic demographic questions, but other variables that capture the complexity of this market because of the existing cultural variations within the Hispanic market that can have an impact in the business proposition. The research companies were asked to select which, among a list of eleven variables, they would consider including in the study on behalf of the hypothetical client. The variables included the basics: age, gender and socio-economic status, and Hispanic market specific questions such as adaptation, acculturation, country of origin, family size, educational level, urban/rural setting, intercity/suburban setting, second/third generation, home ownership, car ownership, or other options.

The results suggest that most Hispanic marketing research companies today integrate at least some basic questions about acculturation and adaptation, in addition to age, gender and socioeconomic status. Two-thirds would include measures of country of origin/heritage, family size, and educational level which provide highly valuable insights to target Latino consumers. For example, including in the analysis the country of birth and or number of years of residence in the U.S. can easily indicate which is the correct positioning, message narrative and marketing strategy for a specific product or service. Because some brands are well known in some Latin American countries but are unavailable or unknown in others, the marketing approach would need to be different if the data shows this pattern; in one case it would be an introductory brand strategy or it would be a competitive strategy if the brand is well known.

Sadly, only a few research companies would incorporate "brand health," that is, questions regarding the attitudes towards the brand and category usage, and only a few included self-reported behaviors, such as language preferences by social occasions.

Market differences by acculturation

Closing the survey, a question was posed regarding what market to select for the study plus two other variables, that would indicate the specific level of knowledge of the research companies of the nuances of the different Hispanic markets or DMAs: language usage and preference (Spanish and English) and generation (foreign-born/first generation, second, third plus) per market. Sadly, only a few participating companies could easily identify markets by degree of acculturation or differences regarding proficiency in English or Spanish, which are relevant marketing issues. For example, San Antonio is a far more "acculturated and English-preferred" market than others, such as Houston, a city in the same state, that is much more "Spanish-preferred/dominant" and less acculturated, due to a larger population of new immigrants. These acculturation insights are easily obtainable, highly valuable, and can facilitate the selection of the best Hispanic market target, for example, to test and introduce new products imported from the different Latin American countries.

Voices from Hispanic Data Producers

After the online surveys were received, study participants were asked to reply to two final questions: *"In your opinion, what is the biggest obstacle that your company faces in future marketing research related to Hispanics?"* and, *"What would you suggest should be done to overcome that obstacle?"* Twelve of the 15 respondents offered responses.

The challenges

The open-ended answers to the question point to two major challenges. First, Hispanic research agencies with experienced in-culture staff are an important resource for corporate clients that want reliable data. Understanding the Hispanic culture is crucial. If companies don't understand the Hispanic culture, then they don't know how to ask the relevant marketing questions nor analyze the responses. Second, the challenges posed by the new technologies, the internet, social media, and so forth, will remain, as new research methods and approaches are developed. One respondent's answer sums up the issues: *"It's not just about telephone surveys or traditional focus groups. The emergence of younger, bi-cultural Hispanic consumers requires more research with social media and nontraditional options (such as video diaries and blogs). It also requires not taking a Spanish-only approach."*

The solutions

As to solutions, the marketing researchers had several suggestions. First and foremost is client education, which would include lessons learned from the brands that are already successful with Hispanic consumers. They can show clients the potential Return on Investment, and benefits of using more ethnographic studies among Hispanic neighborhoods and households. Thought leadership is also important; smaller research companies are already the thought leaders in multicultural research, but this may not be apparent to the corporate world. Finally, smaller companies should invest and create their own research products to improve the representativeness of the samples and panels of Latinos used in marketing research. It may take a consortium of the smaller companies to do that. There was over all agreement that person-to-person interactions are considered necessary for assuring comprehensive and reliable data to include the voices of Latino consumers who are Spanish-language dependant, and less acculturated, and excluded in some research approaches.

Views from Corporate Clients

Four executives from corporations that rely on Latino marketing research data were interviewed to provide the voice of the corporate Hispanic marketing data user. The interviews were conducted via telephone with the following executives:

Jorge Calvachi, Consumer and Markets Insight Manager, Amway Global;

Javier Farfan, PepsiCo Senior Director, Cultural Branding;

Tom Gee, Director, Market Research, News America Marketing; and

Jessica Pantanini, Chief Operations Officer, Bromley Communications.

They were asked: *"In your opinion, what is the biggest challenge your company faces concerning marketing research related to Hispanics?"* and, *"What do you suggest should be done to overcome that challenge?"*

The Challenges

The common denominator in the answers offered by all four executives focused on the limited consistency and reliability of the data offered by marketing research companies. Jessica Pantanini stated that there is a "lack of consistency across research data," regardless of "segmenting of the audience by language, acculturation, etc." She added there were inconsistencies in the inability to "drill down to individual market levels."

Tom Gee pointed out there is a lot of "misinformation about Hispanic consumers in general." According to him, what people believe about Hispanic consumers is "based on past research, but not necessarily true now given the new research." An example offered was the incorrect notion that "Hispanics don't read newspapers or use coupons." Gee does not know if past research documented that Hispanics didn't use these channels, but it certainly is not the case now as his company is successful with inserts in Spanish-language and English-language newspapers.

Another misconception he mentioned is that Hispanics don't shop at large grocery stores. Gee added that due to the misinformation and lack of awareness on how to best reach Latinos, lots of clients are not aware that they can target Hispanics with new research and data tools available in the market.

Javier Farfan told us that the information obtained from their [research] sources did not adequately address the "hidden" population, i.e., the unacculturated, recent immigrants. More specifically, he said that the research and typical tools used to study Hispanics as consumers are skewed, not holistic, and do not provide "a full picture." Farfan added that the category of Hispanic is evolving, that all people's behaviors (including Latinos) are evolving, but that this dynamic group is difficult to reach due to lack of appropriate data. An example offered was the reality of a more "complex identity," one which the multicultural marketing industry thinks of as differentiated just by language, or just based on ethnicity instead of making it [the views of Hispanic consumers] three or more dimensional with other important factors, too. An added comment was that Latino identity was changing due to hyper-local activities, a process that contributes to a lack of a unified Latino identity. To face that reality, a "*more* sophisticated perspective is needed" because "the media platforms out there are not sophisticated enough."

This theme of the complexity of the Hispanic market was addressed by Jorge Calvachi, who said that marketing companies do not know how to target Hispanics within or across groups—a task that is challenging given the diversity of Latinos from different countries. For some issues, for example, Colombians are different from Mexicans, and some decision makers in the marketing industry do not understand that.

On this topic, Gee asserted that the assumption that Latinos are monolithic and that one decision and approach can reach and affect all Hispanics is incorrect. Thus marketing companies do not know how to use diverse media to best reach Hispanics by origin.

Calvachi added that many goods and services companies don't allot enough funds to pay for high-quality research about Latinos. He also indicated that those clients just want simplistic, basic overall data that is not necessarily representative of the nation's Hispanic population. An outcome is the poor quality data that the Latino marketing research companies gather for them.

Expanding on this view, Calvachi further stated: "A lot of executives want to spend on marketing to Hispanic consumers, but they don't consider spending the money for the research, which is a "disservice to the Hispanic consumer." Of particular concern, he said, is the practice of handing projects to study and assess Latino markets to interns or junior researchers. Each time that happens, the foundation of information from past research studies is lost, and the company's data and Hispanic knowledge goes back to the same, limited understanding of the Hispanic consumer.

From Calvachi's experience, this pattern is common even in companies that have areas or teams dedicated to multicultural research. When data has to be gathered about Latinos, instead of banking on solid foundations, to save money those companies rely on newly hired or less experienced persons who re-invent the wheel. The outcome is that managers in Corporate America end up doing the same [wrong] things all over again. An example he mentioned was a pitch for a particular consumer product that was made to management that required a unique dedicated Hispanic marketing approach but was integrated with the General Market approach.

Aside from the managers' doubts about the value of integration, they would not easily provide the funds needed for the Latino component of the marketing campaign. Moreover, when the Latino campaign was developed, it was assigned to interns or junior partners who did not have the knowledge, cultural skills, and ability to challenge the stale notions about Latinos and engage in the needed sophisticated approaches required for this population.

Calvachi also pointed out that there are General Market research companies that claim to have Latino or Hispanic experts, but such is not the case when the person placed in charge of a project is someone who has limited experience with the diversity of Latino and Latin American populations. The problem emerges when a person is hired and presented as an expert because he or she is from, for example, Mexico, but has not had in-depth experience with the vast diversity and complexity of Latinos in the U.S. He asserts, "(These) Marketing research companies are doing a major disfavor to the entire industry because they don't have experts who can synthesize the ideas for the needs of the clients."

Furthermore, he pointed out that another reason for the current limitations in the field is the lack of proper training in schools and in the marketing research companies. With very few exceptions, universities do not offer courses that deal with the diversity and complexity of Latino markets. This lack is especially notable in the Ivy League schools where Corporate America does most of its top-level recruitment.

Solutions

According to Pantanini, a solution to improve the reliability, consistency, and solid foundation of marketing research about Latinos requires improving the academic education and the in-house company training of the people who engage in the data gathering and interpretations. She suggests that all universities should offer courses—in economics, politics, or sociology, and certainly in marketing and advertising—that are more than just passing lessons about the diversity and complexity of Latinos and their cultures. And if the universities do not, the companies who hire the interns and junior partners should do a better job of training them about Latinos.

Independently of each other Calvachi and Pantanini suggested a bolder solution: major corporations that use marketing data should take the lead and invest large amounts of funds in developing and gathering comprehensive and reliable research data. More specifically, Pantanini suggested the establishment of "a consortium of media and researchers working together to create the principles to properly conduct that research." Acknowledging that the barrier to this goal is competition, it was nevertheless presented as a viable option because "each company offers some differentiation or market corner" that could help "dive deep into the geographic and demographic levels" of Hispanics as consumers and subsequently work together to create better ways of looking at the market. With that collaboration, the consortium could also "leverage the sample" when seeking corporate clients. To make this collaboration possible, Pantanini also suggested sharing costs of gathering the larger, more comprehensive and representative sample of Hispanics. While challenging, this goal, according to her, is "not insurmountable."

Calvachi, who also believes that major corporations should take the bold leadership in this arena, proposed that large corporations work with point-of-sale data providers to obtain more accurate sales data and share the data with all, as this would "go a long way" in improving the knowledge about and marketing to Latinos.

Also of particular interest to Calvachi is research data that reliably shows the return on investment (ROI) with the Latino markets. This was considered a crucial step and one that requires the establishment of a "true analytical machine" [research mechanism].

Still focusing on the need for solid and new leadership efforts, Farfan proposed that Chief Executive Officers and Chief Financial Officers from the consumer packaged goods companies should get involved to monitor the holistic information needed about Latinos. This collaborative effort would make sure that marketing and research companies working as committees would "figure out how to take into account the ever more fragmented world we live in." To this end, there is a need to create new tools to work together to respond to the challenges. He also asserted that there is a need to start "being more innovative," and to look in new directions for fresh ideas. For Farfan, part of the solution involves young entrepreneurs who can develop the new technology to overcome the limitations in collecting and analyzing data.

Implications

First, it seems evident that the still developing field of Hispanic-oriented marketing research takes very diverse approaches to gathering data about and understanding Latino consumers. The divergence in recommended sample sizes, data gathering strategies, and targeted geographic locations for a national study representative of the total U.S. Hispanic population is particularly concerning. How representative would a sample of 300 be for 50 million Hispanics, or 16.5 million Latino households with large families or even several family generations living under the same roof? Which Latino subgroups would be excluded if the studies are conducted in only five locations? How representative would the data about Latinos be if collected only via phone or primarily online?

The open-ended comments offered by the respondents to the online survey and follow-up interview questions attest to challenges and limitations for gathering data about Hispanic consumers. The answers reveal many obstacles faced by their companies and the marketing research industry in general. The mergers and concentration of the industry is one oft-stated concern. Likewise, the lack of fully representative samples and panels of Latinos in marketing research is a common denominator mentioned by the respondents.

The companies that do research about Latino consumers cannot stall the mergers and concentrations. However, they can consider developing and offering leadership, innovative proprietary methods and strategies, as well as the education needed by corporate clients. The views shared by the corporate executives who use Latino marketing research data clearly present the main challenges facing the field; namely, the perceptions and opinions that the marketing data about Latino consumers are unreliable and not representative of the Hispanic population at large. While the reasons for those limitations vary, there is consensus among those executives that bold steps and leadership—be it from the research companies, the top brass of the consumer and service companies, or new entrepreneurs—is needed to collectively overcome the challenges.

Their recommendations to address the needs for more use of and greater availability of better trained Hispanic marketing researchers suggests there is an industry-wide, severe shortage of seasoned experts in this area. Both corporations and universities need to address this urgent issue.

We are highly indebted to the Hispanic Association on Corporate Responsibility (HACR) for their grant to support part of this study and to the Center for the Study of Latino Media and Markets, School of Journalism & Mass Communication, Texas State University-San Marcos for their support and permission to publish excerpts of the study. Thanks to Juan Tornoe, Jessika Gómez-Duarte and Amanda Blease at Cultural Strategies for their assistance with the online survey and follow-up calls to the marketing research companies.

Jumping Over the Digital Divide

Carlos E. Garcia

SVP, Knowledge Networks; Founder, Garcia Research Associates, Inc.,
and Cada Cabeza panel

Yes, It Can Be Done

Online research among Latinos is a perfectly viable methodology if you know what you're doing. There are two key options: opt-in, which is the most common method in the General Market, and the enumeration-based probability "invite-in" panel in either the General or Hispanic markets where if people don't have the internet, they are given it. In the interest of full disclosure, the firm I am now a part of—Knowledge Networks—offers each of these options. But how did we get here?

The paradigm has shifted

When I started my career in consumer research in the Hispanic space, the gold standard for quantitative research was door-to-door. This was the tried and true, solid methodology. We were able to conduct national probability samples, even within targeted communities such as the Latino Market. We drew sample based on Hispanic population density, used maps of randomly drawn sample points, random starting points, knocking on every *nth* door. We did validations in person and by phone. We did it right. The results gave insights that drove decisions that worked in the marketplace.

But the world intervened

Secure buildings, scared homeowners, and random stuff you wouldn't believe. One interviewer stumbled into a high stakes poker game in Chicago and was tied up and held at gunpoint for hours until the game was over and everyone left. Here I thought Al Capone was dead. Another drove his white Econoline van into a neighborhood in East LA and was going door-to-door to do some interviewing and found himself having to dive to the ground to avoid being hit in a drive-by shooting aimed at some nearby gang bangers. And the vehicle being driven by the drive-by shooters? A white Econoline van. So he couldn't even get into his vehicle until the police escorted him away. Did he wander onto a movie set? As a result of incidents like this the willingness to seek out solutions seemed to wane even as the need to hear all Latino voices in research was growing.

Danger ranger

Okay, so sending interviewers into iffy neighborhoods with pockets full of cash incentives was becoming too dangerous, but there was a tantalizingly "clean" option—phone interviewing. Computer Assisted Telephone Interviewing (CATI) done from a central location with random monitoring and close supervision became the norm. To that, we added the Hispanic touch with very carefully designed sample frames that took into consideration population density. We could do random digit dialing (RDD) in high-density areas and Hispanic surname samples (you had to have an obviously Latino name like Garcia or Valdés) in low-density areas based on the Census Bureau's data reports.

Each market has a different mix, so we developed an intensely complex algorithm that included every market with 100,000 or more Latinos and at least one TV and one radio station in Spanish (over 147 and rising— we recently added Honolulu and Anchorage). With this we had to factor in each individual market's quirks, how its population is distributed regarding density, and also consider the demographic and country-of-origin distributions, to come up with a process that produces perfect replicas of the U.S. Latino population as determined by the Census Bureau. The results gave insights that drove decisions that worked in the marketplace.

However, even this solution left out many Latino voices because while this solution was elegant and it generally worked, it excluded the most disadvantaged and the least stable households. Worse, this solution was not inexpensive and therefore, dropping Hispanic research became a tempting solution to tight budgets.

But the world intervened. Again, and in multiple ways.

First, the internet, which was initially developed among the campuses of UCLA, UC Santa Barbara, and Stanford for purposes of purely academic data sharing, took off in ways no one could have imagined.

Second, the phenomenon of the cell phone took off.

Third, there was intense pressure to lower costs on everything. Every household in America seemed to be looking for the good life at the best possible price on everything, which caused tons of jobs to be exported, which exerted even more urgency to seek lower prices. An unquenchable downward spiral put intense price pressure on every corner of our economy, including marketing research.

Finally, our economy, which had been flourishing thanks to a booming housing market and home equity loans that were fueling the good life, crashed. So people no longer had the money for both a standard home phone line and a cell phone.

Not to mention young people who never quite saw the paradigm in the same way as their parents did—to them, a land line is like a manual typewriter, e-mail is old fashioned, watches are just bling, and a smartphone is *de rigueur* if only as an interim step towards the next big thing. Remember when planned obsolescence was considered wild? Now things outlast their utility. I have bins full of old devices that were the hottest thing ever for about six months and are now useful only as doorstops.

But we need data

With all of these various forces playing off against each other, the marketing research world, still in desperate need of reliable data, went online. I have heard guesstimates that as much as 95 percent of all consumer research done in the U.S. is done online, yet the reality is it was only 45 percent (*Honomichl Top 50 Report* published in *Marketing News* in July, 2010). But where does this leave the Hispanic market? In the lurch, it seems. Latinos adopted DVD players and cell phones even faster than their General Market counterparts, but the internet has lagged and for one good reason.

Literacy

Access to education in the U.S. is hardly even. The lower income strata do not get access to the same level of education as the upper classes do, and that means the Latino market here in the U.S. (along with their African-American and Native American counterparts) is dramatically under-educated. Latin America isn't any better; it is far worse. So the bulk of the wave of immigrants to the U.S. we saw in the 1980s and 1990s came here with relatively low levels of education. More than half have less than a high school diploma. Couple that with the tragic drop-out rates we see among our urban youth and you have a large segment of the population that isn't having fun with keyboards or accessing the Library of Congress to study Milton and Cervantes.

Flexibility and Agility

Researchers, particularly those who focus on a minority community, must be extremely flexible in designing a data collection strategy and agile in implementing their sampling plans. It may startle some, but it turns out consumers do not spend their lives waiting to be interviewed about toothpaste or the newest variant of their favorite deodorant or cereal. So we have to play along to catch the consumer, to observe and listen, and we have to do whatever is needed to listen in as objective a way as possible and to their true voices, not some echo or a misleading excerpt or a cleverly edited splice job.

To compound the task, people and their situations don't stay the same, which is both maddening and the reason we researchers stay in business.

Nothing is harder to hit and more tantalizing than a moving target, and companies can't sit back and think they've "solved" the Hispanic market because it's constantly changing and grossly under-researched.

Love and respect

If you really care about the communities whose voice you seek to present to the world, then it makes a difference to you if you purposefully or inadvertently leave out a big chunk of the market; in the case of U.S. Latinos that "chunk" is, as of July 2011, 16.3 percent or 50.5 million people. But, sometimes you do that on purpose. If you want to talk to consumers who use remittance companies to wire money to Mexico, you probably don't seek the upper income acculturated consumers. If you want to talk to people who buy certificates of deposit and mutual funds, you probably don't want to talk to the guys who live in the garage of their cousin's house. But if you want to accurately represent the entire Latino population, then all of the various niches must be included, even if you have to go to ridiculous lengths to find them. The Census Bureau tries hard and even with huge resources, it often fails. Every ten years you can count on two things: a census and lawsuits from the advocacy groups that represent the communities of color because they *know* they were not counted accurately.

Your shift is showing

The second decade of the new millennium finds the data collection world in mid-paradigm shift. Clearly the momentum is in the direction of online research, but the incidence of online penetration among Hispanics is still relatively low and so we find ourselves with three main options whose plusses and minuses have to be balanced:

Online There are, as I said at the outset, two kinds of online. The fastest and cheapest methodology is opt-in where people choose to join the research panel of their own accord, partly to share their opinions but normally just to earn some spare change. However, this approach, with no intervention, naturally skews towards the young, well-educated, females, and higher incomes, and skews away from males, older, poorer, less-educated, and Mexican origin. Another alternative is invite-in where a representative panel using address-based sampling is recruited to achieve a nationally representative panel. In the case of the latter, to be statistically representative of the Latino population and conduct the surveys online, those Latino persons who do not already have online access must be given a netbook or laptop and change their ISP, paid for by the firm recruiting them to the online panel. And you have to be prepared to do a LOT of handholding.

Intercept to online By going to malls and shopping areas, we can reach people who are not online, but give them the same experience as the online respondents and we can offer them as much or as little assistance as they need with the computer. This reaches a very different segment but is limited mostly to the major markets. This means we hit Los Angeles but not Bakersfield; Houston but not McAllen; Miami but not Homestead; Chicago but not Springfield. And all in-person work is relatively expensive, especially for low-incidence studies. As a stand-alone, intercept work is useful but not projectable.

Phone Still a viable tool to reach older respondents especially and the smaller markets such as Spokane, Little Rock, Midland/Odessa, Hartford, Salinas. The big drawback is the different platform, having to read scales versus showing scales, having to read questions and concepts instead of being able to show package design mockups, visuals, and the entire list for *a ranking.*

There are expensive ways around this, such as recruiting people to participate, sending them materials and then calling back. It works, but it's unwieldy and time consuming.

Hispanics Online?

The biggest challenge to the research world has been the online aspect specifically for the unacculturated Hispanics. There are many online sample providers who can give you access to English-speaking Latinos, but the Spanish-dominant have been a challenge.

Sampling in the Opt-In or Invite-In World

This is one of the trickiest issues when dealing with online research using samples where participation is driven by the respondent and not the researcher.

Way back in the days of door-to-door research, if someone was home and answered the door, they still had the chance to decline to participate, but back then people were nice and would often feel embarrassed to turn down the nice man or woman at the door with a clip board. The door to be knocked on was carefully selected through random procedures and this worked out fairly well and could produce nationally projectable samples that mirrored the Census Bureau.

Not so far back in the days of call center research, the sample was generated by a sample house and transmitted to the call center and given to the researchers to dial. Eventually more of that became automated until it degraded into the horrible predictive dialers whose most unfortunate feature was a one or two second delay from the time the phone was picked up and someone said hello until the operator got on the line. People quickly learned *that* trick and just hung up in the interim. Sadly, in the numbers game of research, it was still efficient. But the point is that it was the researcher that picked the number to call.

To alleviate the sampling problem, you can stratify the invitations to participate in studies by using the data from the profile questionnaires panelists are given an incentive to fill out. The goal is to replicate as closely as possible the total Hispanic market or the segment thereof that is being targeted. And when the actual completed interviews are flowing in, you can close some quotas and keep others open until the study is appropriately fulfilled. In many cases, after-the-fact weighting is done to implement the micro-adjustments necessary so that the study reflects the target.

As a researcher, I hold two tenets as gospel:

1. The goal is to achieve a representative sample so that the results can be projected out to the population at large. Various tools can

be used to achieve this including stratification (via quotas) and weighting, but this isn't easy. It can be expensive to do this right, but why would you even bother to do research if the accuracy of the results is not important?

2. Weighting is an art form. It can be used to fine-tune a study so that the resulting data hums with the resonance and internal consistency of the truth. But there are limits. I was shocked at a conference when a speaker from a highly respected research firm admitted it had taken 9 interviews and weighted them to look like 300 interviews. This infuriates me as a Latino and as a researcher.

Calibration is another method whereby the ideal target is identified, the sample is launched with an understanding that different groups have different response rates, and then the completed interviews are compared with the target and adjusted accordingly. It's a combination of stratification and weighting with a deft touch. And the results give insights that drive decisions that work in the marketplace.

One of the most current methods being used for probability-based sampling of the population is good, old-fashioned snail mail. Address-based samples (ABS) can be pulled from one of the most comprehensive available sample frames, the U.S. Post Office's Computerized Delivery Sequence File (CDSF). This CDSF file consists of 97 percent of the physical addresses in the U.S. It does not depend on the presence of a landline telephone although the addresses can be matched with landline telephone numbers where they exist (it is not yet possible to match cell phone numbers). It can also be matched with names that can be identified as Hispanic surnames. ABS samples can be successfully used to recruit web panel members by "invitation" in the mail (i.e., "invite-in"). When the invitation materials are printed in both Spanish and English, Latinos of all levels of language proficiency have an opportunity to be invited.

When these samples are weighted to correct for non-coverage and non-response issues, usually the benchmark data come from the U.S. Census Bureau's Current Population Survey monthly estimates. Hispanic ethnicity is included in this benchmark data. However, language proficiency is not addressed so if you need to be sure that you have the correct proportions of language proficiency among a Latino sample, you can find this in another benchmark data set, the Pew National Hispanic Survey that reports the proportions of Spanish-dominant, bilingual and English-dominant adults in the United States.

Pew Hispanic Data Regarding Online Issues

One of the most unassailable sources of information about the U.S. Hispanic community is the Pew Hispanic Center. It does good work and has done it for a while so it has longitudinal data as well as in-depth research. A sampling from: *Latinos and Digital Technology* by Gretchen Livingston, Senior Researcher, Pew Hispanic Center, February 9, 2011:

- Latinos are significantly less likely than Whites to have a home internet connection (55 percent vs. 75 percent); this difference persists even if the sample is limited to internet users (85 percent vs. 96 percent).

- Among internet users, Hispanics are less likely to have a home broadband connection (69 percent) than are Whites (84 percent) or Blacks (78 percent).

- Native-born Latinos are more likely than foreign-born Latinos to be online (81 percent vs. 54 percent), to have a home internet connection (71 percent vs. 45 percent), to have a home broadband connection (60 percent vs. 35 percent) and to own a cell phone (86 percent vs. 70 percent).

- Spanish-dominant Hispanics trail bilingual and English-dominant Hispanics in internet use, home internet access, home broadband access and cell phone ownership.

- Forty-seven percent of Spanish-dominant Latinos use the internet, compared with 74 percent of bilingual Latinos and 81 percent of English-dominant Latinos.

- Thirty-seven percent of Spanish-dominant Latinos have a home internet connection, compared with 61 percent of bilingual Latinos and 77 percent of English-dominant Latinos.

- About one-fourth (26 percent) of Spanish-dominant Latinos have home broadband access, compared with about half (52 percent) of bilingual Latinos, and two-thirds (66 percent) of English-dominant Latinos.

- Among Latinos, internet use, home internet use, home broadband access and cell phone ownership are less prevalent at older ages.
- From 2009 to 2010, the share of Latinos aged 18 to 29 who were online jumped from 75 percent to 85 percent, and the share with cell phones rose from 81 percent to 90 percent.
- Among Hispanics, higher levels of educational attainment and household income are linked to higher rates of internet use, home internet access, having a home broadband connection and cell phone ownership.
- Rates of internet use, home internet access and broadband access are similar for Latinos living in urban, suburban and rural areas.

So you can see how tough a job we faced to bring online research to the unacculturated Latinos.

Many have tried

However, few have succeeded thus far. Some of the biggest companies with the deepest pockets have taken this issue on only to fall flat on their faces because they wanted to use their panel members to fulfill quotas of primarily English-speaking survey-takers, Latino or otherwise. But the number of companies making a mad dash at the online Hispanic panel business grows every day along with the knowledge that to have a *real* Latino sample one must include the unacculturated.

Several companies have their own internal panels for their own studies. The list of companies that now provide sample for online research with Latinos also is growing steadily and includes:

U-Samp	Survey Sampling (SSI)
GMI	Empanel Online
Varsity Plaza/Offerwise	Toluna (formerly Greenfield)
Luth	Accurate Field
Opinionology (formerly Western Wats, now part of SSI)	

David's Little Second Cousin

Knowledge Networks took this on and successfully launched Knowledge-Panel Latino.^{SM} So did a small company with no pockets, no bank support, no angel investors but a determination born of desperation. We at Garcia Research took this on because we were frustrated that in our estimation none of the established opt-in online panel firms had been able to do this effectively and with cultural expertise. We realized that we would have to try to take this on by ourselves. So, madly, we did.

- We hired a young Latino online geek who wanted to work in the Hispanic space away from a major software company.
- We brainstormed a name, tested some quantitatively, but settled on one of my favorite family sayings: *"Cada cabeza es un mundo,"* which literally translates to "Every head is a world," but means that everyone sees things his or her own way. And this is part of the cultural idiom of virtually every Spanish-speaking country, a crucial factor. This became *www.cadacabeza.com.*
- We researched platforms and providers, settling on a company called Confirmit that offered us the utilities we needed and were willing to work with us on payments.
- We hired a web development firm in Tijuana to develop a "look" for our site that would resonate with the unacculturated, Spanish-dominant consumer.
- We hired a Latino artist to create a logo that was workable in many different formats, was fun and friendly, and culturally relevant without pandering or condescending.
- We made a huge effort to build this panel with two clear objectives: one was that we *only* did research, no marketing or communications or advertising; the second was that we wanted this to feel like a community, and not just a churn-and-burn research site.
- We added in community information, resources, links to Spanish-language newspapers and TV station sites from around the Spanish-speaking world, education information, and so forth.

- We started recruiting by phone, using our call center and our own RDD system.
- We later brought in outside online recruiters to help us build our panel.
- We developed a referral program to have our respondents bring in their friends and family so they could earn points towards incentives.
- We developed an incentive program whereby our panelist could earn pocket change doing these surveys—not enough to be a job, but just enough to be worth the trouble.
- We started using our connections in the marketplace to develop symbiotic relationships with others doing good stuff in the Hispanic space that we liked and trusted.

Build, Build, Build

The task at hand became building the panel, growing it in numbers so we could actually start conducting studies. But we also knew we had to keep our panelists busy or we would lose them, not to mention needing additional sources of cash to fund this mad enterprise, so we reached out to other sample providers to sell them access to our precious panelists.

Focus on the toughest target

The community that had eluded the research world was the Spanish-dominant, unacculturated Hispanic. So, perversely, that is what we focused on. And, it seems, we tapped into a whole world out there that was actually eager to share their voices and opinions.

The Cada Cabeza panel started to grow

When we reached 5,000, we contacted all of our sample suppliers and they fainted. At 10,000 we sent out a press release and the research buying market reacted positively. And it kept growing, but new problems emerged:

- The hunger for more sample grew. The story of our panel got out in the research world mostly by word of mouth and a few well-timed visits to online research conferences. But this created a bigger and bigger demand that required us to manage the final balance of client demand and panelist burden. Our first fear that Cada Cabeza panelists would be bored was unfounded!

- Recruiters popped up offering to help us build the panel, but their tactics were not always entirely clean and pure, and we have had to formalize the quality controls we had always had and to enforce them with extreme vigilance.

- Fraudsters popped up, too, trying to join the panel, and we've seen ads in Spanish papers asking consumers to pay them $50 and they would show them how to do surveys online and get paid for it. Grrr, yet not unique to Cada Cabeza.

- We discovered a whole phenomenon of people who looked at our site, clicked on the registration page, felt that the enrollment form was long and detailed, so they didn't bother to fill it out. We are working on making the process easier.

- Another phenomenon was people who signed up but never filled out a single survey. Tens of thousands of them. Grrr, yet again. However, it's endemic to the opt-in world. So we developed a process that effectively encourages people to take this seriously. It should not be surprising to anyone who knows Latinos that they respond to the personal touch and become much more engaged if they know that there are real people behind the web page.

- Skews—right off the bat the opt-in panel skewed female and better educated and to the Southeast and Northeast. Hmmm, a panel full of Cuban and Puerto Rican ladies. Not optimal. Slowly more men and Mexican-origin consumers joined, but we are still underrepresented by men, people over age 50, and Mexican-origin consumers. In the invite-in world (KnowledgePanel Latino), this is carefully controlled.

Getting them is good; keeping them is better

Retention was the real problem that emerged as the panel grew. As it grew we were excited, but participation rates were low and at times, we were having a hard time completing studies. We had been so busy selling and so busy growing that we hadn't done enough to stay in touch with our panelists. Remember we were blazing a new trail by being among the first to build a primarily unacculturated Latino opt-in panel. We simply had to learn along the way and adjust, and that journey continues to this day.

Funny, Latinos are remarkably like people. They like to have incentives for doing stuff. We knew this going in, so we set up a point system that was relatively simple, but that still sounded appealing. We set up a benchmark of 1,000 points when panelists would qualify for a $20 reward. We tried online coupon rewards, but that didn't fly. Consumers would try to use them and end up having to pay the difference if what they wanted was priced above $20. Isn't everything? So we broke down and went to a burdensome, but effective, cash reward system and we now send out hundreds of checks at a time, usually twice a week. At some point we may combine our offerings and give them more choices, but it will be *their* choice, not our imposition.

Recruiting and Rivers

Recruiting to panels is a tricky business. The fastest, quickest routes are often the least reliable. You can pay a ton of money and grow the raw numbers of your panel quite quickly, but will they stick to you? Probably not. Another common source is what is called "river sample"— people who respond to those floating invitations that jump into your screen as you browse through a site. The site and the company that arranges the floating ad get paid if you click on the invitation and complete a survey. I fell for that once and was disappointed that an invitation on ESPN.com sent me to a survey that had nothing to do with sports. River sample is cheap and dangerous. It's hard to know who or what you will get, but people use it for "quick and dirty" studies. As a researcher, the very idea makes me squirm.

Recruiting off-line for an online panel is a tough proposition. We prepared ads for Cada Cabeza, and ran a test on radio, but only posted our TV ad on our site. Advertising is expensive and the jump from one medium to another is not easy to inspire. We know some players in the field are doing this, but we are not using TV and radio for now. However, this might change.

"Retention and recruitment are a simultaneous equation."

These words are true for any panel, but among unacculturated Latinos the importance of retention monitoring and experimentation is paramount. We could attract Latinos to Cada Cabeza, yet keeping members was more complex for many reasons. We needed different approaches than those that were similar to the approach for General Market opt-in panels.

To address this we engaged in a multi-pronged attack to:

- Keep on adding **new** panelists.

- Institute and keep up the welcome call process and **not** bother to leave messages as we proved that this was ineffective.

- Speed up the process whereby respondents received their incentive monies. It seems the whole world has Attention Deficit Disorder and we could not take three weeks to get their money to them.

- Reach our inactive panelists in a variety of ways including phone calls, e-mails, and snail mail. This is our reactivation program.

- Our secret weapon is word of mouth. Referrals are the best way we have found to recruit, not just because it is less expensive to us than recruiters, but because the panelists that come to us from their cousins, neighbors, or friends are better panelists. They are more likely to complete surveys and to stay in the panel longer.

Keeping it personal

Ultimately we discovered that the emotional neutrality and anonymity that is so appealing about the internet to Anglos is exactly what makes it off-putting to Latinos. They want to feel connected, to feel that they are interacting with real human beings, to be able to pick up the phone and talk to someone. Here again, this isn't cheap, but the personal touch makes a difference.

Our main pitch to current and potential panelists is that they get to have a voice. They get to *be* the voice for their all-too-often ignored community. If we place the emphasis on the money they can make, they are sure to be disappointed because about the most any panelist can earn is $20 a month. That's a nice little ice cream treat for the kids, maybe a Friday night pizza, but it won't pay your electric bill.

Using our call center

What is quickly becoming a relic of the past, a research call center, has ironically been the secret that has made our online panel really hum. Our operations center has a call center, a coding department, and a group for programming and data processing along with the panel management group. This allows us to:

- Recruit by phone using randomly generated numbers. It's not mightily efficient but it works and if the interviewers are marking time between paid data collection gigs anyway, why not?
- Take inbound 800 number calls from consumers with questions.
- Make outbound welcome calls to new registrants to the panel.
- Call consumers who have recently received incentive checks to make sure the check arrived, to thank them for being panelists, and to encourage them to invite their friends, family, neighbors, and co-workers.
- Call lapsed panelists to encourage them to become active again.
- Call invitees to specific low-incidence studies who have not opened their mail to encourage their participation.

- With all of this, we have to make sure we aren't harassing them, don't call very often, stay in touch without being intrusive. It's a delicate balance.

Quality Controls

One of the biggest issues facing the online research community (and thus the entire research community) is quality control. The big advantage of the internet is anonymity, and the big disadvantage of the internet is anonymity. Releasing the internet into the human experience was like giving free reign to every good and every bad impulse in the human heart. And, as it turns out, one of the impulses that appears to be deeply ingrained into our DNA is the impulse to cheat if people think no one is looking or if they think they can get away with it. And most people think no one is looking in the internet world and that they can get away with it.

Sadly, they're often right. In the General Market, the volume of research that gets done is massive, the panels used are in the millions, and the price pressure on providers is such that there are no budgets to pay people to sit there and check every interview. Instead, a program checks everything for problems. I have had friends who have virtually had their businesses ruined because it was discovered too late that hackers or fakers had made up survey data.

Happily for the Hispanic market, what makes this market segment more work also is our greatest strength. Because Latinos need the personal touch, this forces us to effectively interact with them. We conduct welcome calls, reminder calls, and we even mail checks to their homes. By doing this we incidentally pick up non-Latinos who have faked being Hispanic. We also have found people using fake names or addresses and we have found one person pretending to be several different people. In other words, all of this personal interaction is expensive, but it buys us personal engagement plus a huge opportunity for quality control. We check it out if we make a welcome call and it's a disconnected number or a business. We will send an e-mail asking for a correction and if we don't get it, we purge them from the system.

Automated quality control systems are in place, of course, including:

- Checking for duplicate IP addresses within our database. If this comes up, we can try to verify that it is in fact multiple members of the same household.

- We also check for duplicate addresses for mailing incentives or duplicate phone numbers when people register.

- Checking for duplicate responses in surveys. In one instance, we found 35 surveys with precisely identical responses. Can we say **red flag**?

- Checking for answer patterns. I call this the Bart Simpson (BS) syndrome where people appear to be making patterns in the answer grids rather than actually answering the questions. We can also see where contradictory answers make it obvious the person was not paying attention. Delete.

¿Got Hispanic?

It is important to us that our panel should include only Hispanics. But what does it mean to be Hispanic? How can you prove this? Hispanicity, as I like to call it, doesn't imply any racial characteristics. A Hispanic can be of European, African, Asian, or Native American origin (or any combination thereof). They probably aren't Aboriginal Australian, English Royalty, or Inuit, but who knows? And some people adopt the Hispanic culture by choice (marriage, affinity, a beloved nanny, a good friend, the neighborhood they grew up in, a parent's foreign posting, and so forth).

There are at least 23 countries that are officially listed as being "Hispanic" in that their cultural roots go back to Spain:

1. Spain	9. Cuba	17. Chile
2. Mexico	10. Puerto Rico	18. Argentina
3. Guatemala	11. Dominican Republic	19. Paraguay
4. Honduras	12. Colombia	20. Uruguay
5. El Salvador	13. Venezuela	**21. Equatorial Guinea**
6. Costa Rica	14. Bolivia	22. Philippines
7. Nicaragua	15. Peru	23. United States
8. Panama	16. Ecuador	

Note that everything seems normal on this list until you get to the bottom. Equatorial Guinea is a teensy country, smaller than Boise, Idaho. The Philippines was conquered by Spain and won its freedom in 1898, so it is perhaps the most tenuous of inclusions, but some still speak Spanish and relish their historical ties to Spain. In fact, an ex-president of the country was a gentleman (a wonderful man, I hope) named Carlos Garcia.

But perhaps the biggest surprise on the list is the United States. Yes, the U.S. is the third largest Spanish-speaking country in the world, and at 50 million + and growing, births have replaced immigration as the single biggest source of the growth of the Hispanic population.

For us, a big complicating but elemental factor is acculturation. In the U.S. there are virtually infinite levels of acculturation that come into play, and whether someone is a newly arrived immigrant in the Bronx who speaks only Spanish or someone whose relatives arrived with the Conquistadores in New Mexico and speaks only English, whether they sit on the Supreme Court, do brain surgery, pick tomatoes, or make tacos in a truck parked by the side of the road, they are Hispanic. They can have names like Gomez or Roybal-Allard, and they are Hispanic.

So it's a bit of a judgment call. We can ask people if they consider themselves to be Latino and why, what aspect of the Latino culture do they particularly identify with, and we pretty much have to content ourselves with that and try to guilt people into confessing rather than applying any particular litmus test that would have to vary from country to country and would only be approximate in any case.

If they don't have the internet, give them the internet

This is the "invite-in" model used by Knowledge Networks (KN). KN's approach is to use an ABS frame to produce a probability-based web panel. In the random-digit dialing (RDD) Spanish-language supplemental sample, for those households where an address can be matched to the RDD telephone number, a bilingual advance letter is mailed to facilitate cooperation. Those Latino households that do not have access to the internet at home are given a netbook at the point of recruitment. In Spanish-dominant households, the netbook is configured in the Spanish language. If there were other companies using this same technique (or anything even vaguely similar) I would include them here but for now, *nada*. I just hope others will see the potential in the Hispanic space.

This is essentially the approach taken by Nielsen when it creates its TV ratings panels, but instead of installing people meters that track what TV stations are being watched and who is watching them, KN gives them a netbook and an internet connection.

Garcia Research was involved in the implementation of this approach. We did the call center work to find people and recruit them to join the panel. We also do what is called prompting and retrieval, which means if people haven't been doing surveys despite repeated invitations, they get a call to remind them of their role in the panel. If they choose at this or any point to drop out of the panel, they are asked to send the laptops back to KN.

KnowledgePanel Latino (KPL) has been successfully introduced into the market, most heavily used for segmentations, opportunity, media, brand communication, and awareness and use (A&U) studies by government agencies and academic institutions. This panel and the Cada Cabeza panel are now under one roof, so the two can be used separately or together using the calibration approach.

But not all Latinos are online or want to be online

There is this reality—many Latinos are techno-phobic. They fear something that demands a high degree of literacy, and if they have a limited education it can be intimidating. Then there is the generational factor. Many in the older generations simply don't like any of this digital hoohaa. They didn't grow up with it, they don't get it, and it's like you asked a teenager to have all his teeth removed and wear dentures instead. Just no. And then there are those who simply don't like the internet. They find it impersonal, full of scams and spam, threats and ugly stuff. So with these very legitimate obstacles, it is pretty hard to get some Latinos to play in the online sandbox. Yet even with all of these obstacles, the panel efforts described here prove that it can be done.

Please note that there are some populations that don't participate in any survey using any methodology no matter what, including:

- High wealth individuals;
- The insanely busy such as business owners, single Moms, and high-powered executives;
- People who truly believe that no one could possibly really care about their opinion and thus don't buy into the concept;
- People who are horribly intimidated by the process—the paranoid, sociopaths, people with even mild mental health issues, and shut-ins;
- People who feel they are above the process such as the arrogant, the aloof, misanthropes, and the truly unpleasant personalities.

Combining modes and methodologies

Some researchers are extremely wary of mixed methodologies, and with reason. Different modes or methodologies can yield very different results simply by the nature of the presentation. The same respondent can answer an oral question in a very different way than a written question. An in-person interview necessarily involves person-to-person interaction, and this can be a good thing or a bad thing, but the key is that it introduces a wild card variable. Did the interviewer's pleasant demeanor and attractive appearance influence the responses? Did a young, arrogant, and slightly abrupt young man with baggy pants alienate older, personally conservative respondents?

All that is true, and yet, given the various strata of the Latino population, ranging from the super-assimilated financiers to the day laborers, from suburban housewives to the urban school cafeteria workers, we need to have a way to include the voices of very diverse elements of our wonderful and multifaceted Latino community.

- So if you want to reach seniors, is online an option? Probably not the best choice for opt-in but possible on a probability-based online panel. How about phone? Well, yes, that could work.

- If you want to reach young people, is phone an option? Probably not. They don't have landlines; cell phones are a clumsy option, and they're never home. Online? Yes.

- If you want to reach day laborers and bus boys and gardeners, is online an option? Probably not. Is phone an option? Probably not. Is in-person an option? Yes.

- Strong arguments can be made and data can be produced that suggests that the enumeration-based approach can work even with the least acculturated, but some clients remain skeptical.

One way to reach people who can't be reached online to create an opt-in online panel is to do intercept-to-online. You can specifically screen for targets you can't reach online. You can screen out people who are reachable online. You can give those you can't reach online an interview experience that essentially is the same as the online environment because the interview *is* online (on a laptop with a Wi-Fi or cell internet connection).

But for intercept-to-online to be reliable, you need to use reliable field services that know the market, who have trained interviewers, who have facilities or arrangements for physical set ups that make the process possible, verifiable, and valid. These field services tend to be found in major markets only, so we can get spectacular coverage of Los Angeles, New York, Chicago, Miami, Houston, and some smaller markets like San Diego, Albuquerque, Fresno, San Antonio and Tampa. But that still means you are leaving out a huge number of smaller cities like Salinas, McAllen, Hartford, Peoria, Milwaukee, Las Cruces, and Saratoga.

Different Categories, Different Methodologies

As I mentioned above, different categories have different realities in the Hispanic landscape. As a researcher who wants and needs to be nimble and flexible to find the right people to answer the right questions, you have to adapt your methodology to your category.

Obviously any low-incidence study is always more of a challenge, which may lead you to sample in alternative ways but any specialized product category will have the same issue. For example:

- If you need to talk to women who are undergoing chemotherapy for breast cancer, then you might want to go through oncologists to reach them (of course the HIPAA rules must be respected). More common conditions like diabetes or obesity can be researched online.

- If you want to talk to new car purchasers of a particular brand, you might need a list company that can, in some states at least, provide you with names of people who have registered a new car. (California does not permit this ever since a starlet was murdered by a stalker who got her home address this way.)

- If you want to reach users of specific remittance services, you might need to post interviewers outside their retail outlets.

- If you want to do a study on how illiterate or nearly illiterate parents can help their children perform at school, then online is probably not an option, but you can do intercept-to-online where you can offer people as much assistance as they might need. Phone would probably cost way too much for a low incidence issue like this.

- Reaching the unbanked may require an intercept approach as il-literacy can be a barrier to banking and the unbanked population is less likely to be online or to have a landline.

- Very sensitive topics like feminine protection, STDs, erectile dysfunction, contraception use and drug use can be more easily researched online. This is where the anonymity helps. Most Latinos would rather set their hair on fire than talk to someone about these very personal matters.

However, if the incidence is above 15 percent or so, it becomes more cost effective to use more random techniques that might not be inexpensive, but would be much more projectable. Any standard study on insurance, amusement parks, alcoholic beverages, or virtually any consumer packaged goods can easily be researched online.

Conclusion—For now

The absolute ideal would be to have teams, perhaps of college students, trained, equipped, and ready to go to bring the online surveys to respondents and to be able to offer them as much or as little assistance as they need to complete the survey. This would complement our carefully stratified online sample and make augments available for KnowledgePanel Latino. Finally, there would be a new gold standard to provide results that reveal insights that drive decisions that work in the marketplace. But everything is always changing, and the trick is to keep up.

The Future

We now know better than to trust any paradigm for too long, so what might the future hold? Several enterprises are working on the next big thing, and there are several worth keeping your eye on, including:

Mobile apps for smart phones. Companies can send short surveys to persons who agree in advance to respond to invitations so they can check their app and go to a quick survey. This obviously would skew to the young, the slightly higher income folks and the tech savvy, but that can be a good thing for the right survey. The limitations are the length of the survey and the kinds of visuals you can present.

As TV slowly creeps online and with the advent of fiber optic systems that can support interactivity, it will be possible in the future to do instant polling on any topic. The trick will be to pre-arrange or incent participation without building in any particular skew. As the fiber optic systems are relatively rare now, it will be a while before this filters out to the whole country and covers more than the upper and middle classes.

Online qualitative research is increasingly common, but this may expand even more for certain communities. For the Hispanic market this is still a rarity but will no doubt grow.

Programs for feedback are fairly common, but for now most involve taking your receipt home, going online, and filling out a survey. Surely something faster and easier will crop up, like little touch screen polling stations—iPoll?

The fly on the social media wall. Companies are now in the process of establishing procedures for keeping an eye on the chatter in the social networks and blogosphere. Some think this is a cleaner read of consumer behavior without any "observed behavior bias" but others find it to be a scary Big Brother intrusion into their personal lives. Somehow this will be worked out to function without undue intrusion. But how this would apply to Latinos is not clear, as the penetration of Latinos into the social media is still relatively low. However, Pew suggests this is growing fast. The marketing research industry will no doubt find ways to take advantage of these observational opportunities and to integrate them into their market metrics.

Final Words: Online Research — ¡Sí Se Puede!

Knowledge Networks specializes in innovative online research that gives leaders in business, government, and academia the confidence to make important decisions. With its 2011 acquisition of Garcia Research Associates, KN has 15 full-time staff in its Hispanic research team, as well as unmatched panel resources for accessing all facets of the U.S. Hispanic population. *www.knowledgenetworks.com*

Social Metrics that "Matter"—
Deepening Brand Connections through Social Impact

Derene Allen

Adjunct Professor, Business School, University of San Francisco

Managing Partner, SSG, Multi-Cultural Business and Marketing

THERE are some things we do because we have to, others because we want to, and others we do, well, just because it's the right thing to do.

Then there are those few opportunities where we have a convergence of motives. Perhaps the time has come when by implementing social impact programs that benefit the communities where we do business and by telling the stories of those individuals whose lives we have positively impacted or even transformed through these programs, we strengthen our brand. This turns these endeavors not only into programs that are the right thing to do, but also becomes something we *must* do to deepen the connection to our brand and ultimately our financial results.

As business professionals, we are familiar with financial indicators such as revenue, units sold, cost of goods sold (COGS), EBITDA, ROI, and the proverbial bottom line.

But how do we track, among other things:

- Employee volunteerism;
- Number of employees hired who have had a recent history of un-stable housing, incarceration, substance abuse issues, and so forth;

- Efforts to assist battered women to be able to support their families;
- Research for diseases that plague our different communities;
- Helping troubled teens learn positive leadership skills and avoid gang or other negative environments;
- Reduction of your carbon footprint: fewer pounds of waste sent to our landfills;
- Redesign of product packaging to be more planet friendly;
- A re-engineered distribution system to have less of an impact on our earth; or
- Redesign of your manufacturing process to be more ergonomically friendly to reduce repetitive motion disabilities.

The metric for social impact programs and the corresponding financial indicator generated as a result of these programs could be units sold as a result of doing good in the community or dollars returned to the business' bottom line as a result of giving back to a community. The metric could also be the impact on brand image, brand loyalty, or brand advocacy, but these factors are still, more difficult to measure. With so many cost pressures, reduced headcount, efficiency requirements, and competition at a global level, it is difficult to think about adding anything more to our existing plate full of challenges and headaches. Why does this matter anyway?

Because consumers care

To "start a conversation" on this topic, an online survey was conducted in September 2011 as a directional "pulse" on the market. Out of more than 120 respondents across the nation age 16 and over, more than three-quarters responded that "a company's actions in giving back to the community are very important or somewhat important, when deciding on purchasing a product or service," with over one-quarter saying it was "very important."

Over two-thirds (68 percent) of those same respondents said that knowing that a company gives back to the community is much more or more important today than it was one year ago, and 78 percent said that it is much more or more important than it was 5 years ago.

Over 50 percent said they would be willing to pay for a company's social impact programs, with another 37 percent saying, "maybe." How much more? Three-fourths said between 5 and 10 percent more. Prior experience has shown us that while consumers say this, often their actions do not reflect it. However, their responses do show that they are *thinking* about it, so as marketers, we need to help them *act* upon it. We need to leverage these altruistic impulses to establish a deeper consumer connection and perhaps build competitive advantage.

Looking at responses from Hispanics that participated in the study, they are even more likely (82 percent) to say it is very or somewhat important for a company to give back to the community. Forty-three percent said they would be willing to pay more for a product offered by a company with a strong reputation for giving back to the community. Again—*thinking* about it. Yet in-market experience has yet to prove that they act on it. A study developed by Georgetown University's Center for Social Impact Communication and Olgilvy & Mather with a nationally representative sample of 2,000 respondents (data gathered November-December 2010), corroborates that social causes are important to many Americans, with 45 percent of all Americans aged 18+ involved in a cause. And, there are statistical differences showing that Hispanics and African Americans are *more likely* to be involved with a cause, with 53 percent of African Americans, 52 percent of Hispanics, and 42 percent of Caucasians being involved in a cause.

Impact on the multicultural population

It is likely that multicultural populations are more inclined to be involved in a cause because their communities are the most impacted, and as such, community action has almost become a part of their culture. According to the 2010 Census, poverty surged to its highest level since 1993, median household income declined, leaving the typical American household earning less in inflation-adjusted dollars than it did in 1997. Children were particularly affected, with 22 percent living in poverty. For White non-Hispanic children the percentage living in poverty was just above 12 percent. For Black children, this share is 40 percent. More than one-third of Hispanic children lived in poverty, and they account for 37 percent of all U.S. children in poverty.

So whereas our multicultural communities may be closer to those in the community who need a hand up, many who are a part of the community are financially impacted themselves, and cannot afford the "luxury" of paying more for a product or a service that supports their community more.

Generational differences

Looking at this "conversation starter" data by generation we see some interesting trends. Two-thirds (68 percent) of Boomers, born between 1946 to 1964 say knowing that a company actively gives back to the community is very or somewhat important in making a purchase decision, whereas 78 percent of Gen X (born between 1965–1981) and 83 percent of Gen Yers (Millennials, born between 1982–1996) say so. One-third of Boomers, 47 percent of Gen Xers and a whopping 70 percent of Millennials say they would be willing to pay more for a product offered by a company that has a strong reputation for giving back to the community. Our multicultural populations, particularly Hispanics, skew younger, and are proportionally a larger portion of these younger age segments. Once again, we see a message that younger generations are more attuned and thinking even more strongly about this.

This top of mind "radar" is signaling an apparently growing trend over time that the market is increasingly more conscious about a company's social impact in the community and this is important in making purchasing decisions. The new generations of consumers, and within this group, Hispanic consumers, are saying so at a greater level.

Doing good is not enough

As far back as 2006, consumers were saying that positive social attributes in a product or service are important and that some would pay more for these. However, they will *only* do so when the functional attributes of these products or services meet their needs. Doing "good" is not sufficient alone to encourage purchase (*Stanford Social Innovation Review*, Stanford University, Fall 2006).

The responses to the survey conducted as background for this chapter, are directionally so consistent that it is valid to ask whether, as growth-focused enterprises, we just want be part of this conversation or do we want to be advocates of this movement, leading by example? It appears that we are seeing a market "request" (across segments) for companies to contribute more to the communities in which they operate. But when will Consumer Social Responsibility kick in to match the Corporate Social Responsibility? When will consumers not only *think and say* that they would like to support brands that support the community more *and* even pay more for them, but actually *act* on it?

Digging deeper

Consumers are ever more educated, ever more demanding and exacting. The "transparency bar" on what companies are doing "for the community" has been raised with consumers asking companies what exactly they are doing for the community and what portion of the funds raised are really going to the cause.

Respondents to our survey were asked in what types of community activities they are looking for companies to actively participate. The types of causes varied from breast cancer to education for underprivileged children.

Most interesting were some of their verbatim responses to the question: "What information do you look for about how companies give back to the community?" Here are a few:

"I want to understand how the program works, the impact in the community that they are helping."

"Actual value of contribution versus public relations value—is the action just for publicity value?"

"I'd like to know how they are helping versus 'we support xxx.' Specifics on how the companies are helping charities or communities make it more personal. Any corporation can write a check to a charity and say, 'We're helping.'"

"Authenticity, rather than just a public relations approach. Try to see how the company treats its own workers, vendors."

"Proof that they are actually helping the community and committed to the issues they claim to support."

"I look for a company that is proactive, making it part of their mission (to give back to the community) rather than supporting United Way."

"Proof that their claim is legitimate. Independent reports on how helpful the company is.

"Being a trend-setter, influencing other companies to be good corporate citizens."

In summary, what the community seems to be saying is, "token efforts are not welcome."

Some companies are getting it right

Over three-fourths of respondents said they had purchased a product from a company they knew was giving back. Companies like Target, General Mills, Macy's, Seventh Generation, and Tom's Shoes were mentioned for reasons like: Profits are donated back to the community; Box Tops for Education; their packaging has less impact on the environment.

Respondents found out that companies were doing these things in various ways: by reading about it online or in a newspaper, clear labeling on the package, seeing it in the store, an activity at their child's school, or word of mouth. In other words, these companies also communicated to the consumer that they were doing this activity in the community. Some commonalities stood out. Among those companies cited, respondents said their cause or community activity was very tangible and memorable, and in many cases, local.

Education, health and job creation

From Hispanic respondents, causes most often cited as important to them revolved around education, health, and job creation. The brands mentioned, as those from whom they have purchased, support those causes in their community, and are those who *have a presence in the community*, either as retailers (i.e., Target) or their brands are distributed at local retailers and target Hispanic consumers in-culture (i.e., General Mills).

With causes that are near to the Hispanic community's heart such as education, a local presence and local relevance are indispensable. In this age of social media, word of mouth, face to face is still the most common way of communicating information about causes for Americans across generations. Sixty-two percent of Americans say that being told in person, "face to face," is the way they are most commonly informed about causes in which others want them to be involved. African Americans and Hispanics are more likely to believe they can get the word out about a cause through online social networks. Gen Y and Gen X also report using social media more than older generations for both receiving and sending messages about causes (Ogilvy PR and Georgetown University's Center for Social Impact Communication, Study 2010).

Social impact metrics to track

Whatever the community cause most relevant to your business and brand *and* to the communities in which you operate, America's consumers seem to be asking for social impact programs that are:
- Local
- Tangible
- Committed (where you as a company are "accountable" and the community knows it)
- Clearly communicated, with all the details

Start now, even if on a small scale. Our youth are coming out of college in a tough job market. Corporations can provide internship opportunities and harness the strength that inter-generational endeavors provide. Poverty is at an all time high and corporate management can give employees incentives to volunteer. Choose a cause that *fits* your brand and be consistent and sincere.

Recently, while on a tour of a call center in San Antonio, Texas, I noticed posters and cause activities written on a big wall calendar in the cafeteria:

Food Drive!

Walk to end Alzheimer's!

I asked the company representative why they were so involved in different community activities. She responded, "These suggestions come from our telephone reps. When you deal with the public, you see how much need there is in the community, and you want to give back."

With increasingly challenging economic times, the weight of both Corporate Social Responsibility and Consumer Social Responsibility cannot fall solely on the shoulders of one or the other. Both parties need to do more with less. To accomplish this, bilateral innovation is required.

As *consumers*, if we want to support brands that do more for our communities and our environment, we need first to know about these and to find a way within our personal means to support them.

As *corporate marketers*, if we want to meet the consumer request to be more socially responsible, we will need to find new efficiencies so that we can incorporate community causes into our brand's essence, without significantly impacting the end cost to our customers.

The brands that manage to do this, along with the other guiding principles of providing your customers with social impact activities that are: local, tangible, committed, and clearly communicated will win over the hearts, minds—and pocketbooks—of today's consumers. Across communities. Across generations.

Using the metrics

The data that demonstrate the positive link between doing "good" in the community and strengthening one's brand is growing. The Center for Corporate Citizenship at Boston College reported in its 2010 Corporate

Social Responsibility Index that companies that invest in social initiatives are also investing in building reputations and creating support from their stakeholders, by demonstrating the linear relationship between scores on corporate social responsibility and corporate reputation.

The future of social impact metrics is that they will become part of the company's DNA, involving the community in the conversation from day one. The next generation of consumers and employees, will not ask *if* a company should have a social impact agenda, they will say, "*Of course, it must and we will make it happen.*"

Don't rely solely on this "conversation" to make your decision on becoming involved in generating social impact metrics for your brand and deepening your brand connection. Talk to your customers, your communities. Let them tell you about what "matters" to them. Most important, start the conversation.

Futurecast: Thoughts from the field

After linking your brand to a social cause that increases brand value and loyalty, what comes next? What can be learned from our not-for-profit peers? Seasoned social impact practitioners were asked their perspective on the future direction of social impact initiatives and metrics to complement the consumer perspective on the importance of giving back to the community.

For-profit and not-for-profits are beginning to converge

In the past, the focus for not-for-profits was on counting the number of "people" helped. Now they are experiencing increased pressure to look at profitability. For this, they turn to their for-profit counterparts.

In the future, these experts see younger generations driving this convergence of business and social agendas. They will drive a relational supply chain, demanding a social impact agenda, and create that multiplier effect so it becomes socially normal. Here is what some thought leaders told us:

"The future is a public/private partnership, driven by a need for consistency and market acceptance of social impact metrics. Financial metrics have been defined for years, like GAAP (Generally Accepted Accounting Principles); social impact metrics need to arrive at this level of sophistication and standardization," says Antonio Aguilera, Board Chair of the Social Enterprise Alliance, San Francisco Bay Area Chapter.

Deb Goldberg is general manager of Natural Home Cleaning Professionals based in Oakland, California, and voted 2009 Best Small Business in the California 9th District and *San Francisco Gate* Best in the Bay for 2008 and 2010. She runs a worker-owned cooperative providing jobs for low-income women, many of whom are Latinas, and a triple bottom line business (people, profit, planet). Deb envisions a future where "we track what the impact is on the children of these women, now that their mothers have a stable income: what percentage graduate from high school, pursue college studies, navigate childhood challenges (like staying out of gangs), and fundamentally have ambitions in life and really achieve something."

Steve Hicken, economic development director of Catholic Charities, one of the largest not-for-profits of Santa Clara County, sees in the future "tracking the reduction on the draw of social services once people have steady employment and a stable income (reduction of usage of government provided housing, medical services, food stamps, etc.)." Smiling, he also noted, "It would be nice to be able to create a metric on prosperity and contentment—people having a full and complete life. What is enough?"

Juma Ventures is an innovative and award-winning youth development program that combines employment in social enterprises, college preparation, and financial and intellectual asset building to create a safe, supportive community where under-resourced youth can achieve their dreams of a college education. Marc Spencer, CEO, envisions "tracking the impact on the community at a macro level and not just on the individual or micro level. How many youth of color are rising up, completing college and returning to their communities, opening businesses, going into politics, and becoming educators?"

How do the multicultural markets fare in this Futurecast? Like more traditional companies, until there is a real need to look at the market by cultural sub-segment, it is not a must have on the social metrics radar. Initiatives come to the forefront only if they don't work. For example, many healthcare or potable water initiatives have failed because specific community needs were not taken into consideration. Many neighborhoods continue to be mired in poverty despite initiatives from some of the brightest minds at top-class universities and countless do-gooders.

Maureen Sedonaen, of Revolution Foods, who believes all students should have access to healthy, fresh food on a daily basis, says, "It is a daily consideration to make sure kids eat their healthy lunches. Low sodium, high fiber, brown rice and beans are not as "tasty" as the usual white rice and beans cooked in pork lard, so it is critical to add a "cultural" factor, such as a local hot sauce, to give it "flavor." She laughs, "The challenge then becomes for the school to allow it; some having said that the hot sauce packet makes too much mess, so they don't want to serve it. Then the students don't want to eat their lunch! These are the details that make or break an initiative."

So let's add that "hot sauce" to our social impact metrics! Spice things up, and make a difference!

Santiago Solutions Group (SSG) is a thought leader in strategy and management consulting, creating innovative multicultural business strategies. SSG's strategic framework focuses on quantifying the core target segments' upside revenue potential vis-à-vis its acculturation trigger points through an array of proprietary methodologies. Its 5-P's strategic blueprints empower corporate planning and marketing teams, as well as ad agencies, to conceive multicultural programs capable of sustaining traction. *www.santiagosolutionsgroup.com*

Acknowledgments

THIS BOOK, *WIN! the Hispanic Market: Strategies for Business Growth*, is possible thanks to the incredible support of nineteen friends and colleagues who despite their terribly busy lives and schedules contributed chapters or POVs (Points of View) to make this game-changing book a reality. I am indebted to each of you not only for your passion and belief in the "book project," and the need to elevate the Hispanic market in this new era, but also for sharing your insights and expertise with such candor and generosity. Gracias, muchas gracias! Thanks to each of you, Steve Moya, Carlos Orta, Michael Klein and David Wellisch, Alison K. Paul, Jessica Pantanini, Marie Quintana, Gabriela Alcántara-Diaz, Don Longo, César Melgoza, Doug Darfield, Roberto Orci, Lee Vann, Lucia Ballas-Traynor, Martha Montoya, Federico Subervi, Carlos Garcia, and Derene Allen.

A special shout-out to to my very dear friend and former business partner, Carlos Santiago, not only for your rich and comprehensive chapter that brings to life the complicated process of "sizing the Hispanic business opportunity" with such elegance, but also for the great enthusiasm, support, and generosity you have given the book, and me. I could not have brought the "book project" to life without your valuable insights, suggestions, and on-going encouragement. My gratitude is deep and abiding.

I am hugely indebted to Carlos Orta, ED, HACR, for his generous permission to use portions of the HACR-sponsored Hispanic Marketing

Research Study, and to Professor Federico Subervi, Ph.D., Director of the Center for the Study of Latino Media & Markets, School of Journalism and Mass Communications, Texas State University-San Marcos who directed the study. This seminal industry study provided the base for Chapter 5 and has inspired many in the Hispanic marketing research trade to take a deeper look, review and set standards to improve those areas of concern uncovered by the HACR/TSU study.

Very special thanks to Jorge Calvachi, Javier Farfan, Tom Gee, and Jessica Pantanini for agreeing to participate in the Hispanic primary research study.

Many thanks to Doris Walsh, "partner in crime" editor extraordinaire, and my publisher, Jim Madden, at Paramount Market Publishing. Because of your support I was able to dream this project and because of your help I could make it happen and bring the book to completion! Your contributions are enormous and my gratitude is beyond words.

Thanks to the many friends and colleagues at PepsiCo, Frito-Lay, and Quaker Oats for providing me with endless opportunities to learn from you and your leadership, especially Indra Nooyi, who has inspired me with a novel perspective to think of the business world: "with positive intent," so many thanks! My thanks to John Compton, Al Carey, Massimo D'Amore, Jose Luis Prado, Ron Parker, and Maurice Cox (my first PepsiCo client more than 20 years ago), and beloved Becky "Mama Hen" Moore for your trust, friendship, and support all these years.

To dear friends, the Honorable Arabella Martinez, Cecily Drucker, Orlando Padilla, Carlos Orta, Marcela Medina and the Honorable Aida Alvarez for your insights, feedback, and support, my eternal thanks!

Last but not least, thanks to my parents for the values they shared and instilled in me and for teaching me to focus on "The Greater Good," and to my little family for bringing so much love and sweetness to my life. Thanks from the bottom of my heart.

SAN FRANCISCO
NOVEMBER 16, 2011

M. Isabel Valdés

M. Isabel Valdés is a visionary marketer and consumer insights expert. She popularized integrated multicultural marketing through *In-culture marketing* and *Marketing for Share of Heart*, that are gold standards in business and marketing today. She is passionate and committed to bring Hispanic marketing to corporate America and to bring Corporate America to the Hispanic community.

An accomplished entrepreneur, she founded Hispanic Market Connections, Inc., an award-winning marketing research and consulting company, which was sold and publicly traded in 1998. Presently she heads IVC In-Culture Marketing, Transforming Heart Shares into Market Shares,™ strategic marketing consultancy. She is a member of PepsiCo and Frito-Lay's Ethnic Advisory Board and heads its Human Sustainability Committee.

An active community leader she has served as trustee on several national and regional Hispanic community organization boards, including, NCLR, (The National Council of La Raza,) D.C., The National Hispana Leadership Institute, (D.C.) The Tomas Rivera Policy Institute, Los Angeles, and she co-chairs the Mexican Heritage Corporation, in San Jose.

She has received numerous honors and awards, including being selected by *Fortune* Small Business as a "Woman Entrepreneur Star," and

"Business Woman of the Year" by the New York Hispanic Chambers of Commerce. She was named "21st Century Star of Multicultural Research" by *American Demographics* magazine.

For almost a decade she was a lecturer at the Summer Executive Communications Series and the Business School at Stanford University, her alma mater. She frequently speaks at trade conferences, in C-Suites, and at universities.

This is her fifth book, her first as an editor.

Ms. Valdés shares her time between San Francisco, California and South America.

About the Contributors

Steve Moya, senior adviser at Santiago Solutions Group, has decades of high level expertise in strategy, marketing, segmentation and public relations/communications, having assisted businesses and non-profits with growth strategy and marketing, as well as leading organizations to advance innovation. Prior to joining SSG, Steve was senior vice president chief marketing officer of Humana responsible for marketing, corporate communications and government relations and actively involved in corporate strategy development. Before joining Humana he was vice president of strategic planning and communications for Austin-based LatinWorks Marketing and a principal with Growth Strategies Consulting. Earlier in his career, he co-founded one of the largest and most respected ethnic public relations firms in the country, Moya, Villanueva & Associates, which was sold to Manning, Selvage and Lee, an international communications company where he served as a senior vice president.

Michael Klein is co-founder and managing partner of the Latinum Network, a business network specifically designed to help brands reach U.S. Hispanics. Prior to founding Latinum, Mr. Klein was an executive director with the Corporate Executive Board, the leading global provider of executive networks and B2B shared content services. Mr. Klein held a number of senior positions there, most recently running the Strategy and Management Practice. In this role, he was responsible for building and managing the world's largest networks for chief strategy officers and divisional presidents, and was a frequent speaker at corporate leadership and strategy summits around the world. He also ran the Human Resources Practice and was a senior member in the Financial Services Group.

David Wellisch is the co-founder of the Latinum Network. Prior to this, David was the founder and general manager of AOL Latino and was a senior executive in the strategy and business development group. While at AOL, he originated the concept behind AOL Latino and was responsible for the entire operation, overseeing programming, product development, customer service, marketing, strategy, and business development. He has been widely recognized for his work in the industry, and, in 2005, was selected as Hispanic Marketer of the Year by *AdWeek*'s Hispanic Edition. David has also had senior positions at Allied Capital and Gemini Consulting.

Carlos F. Orta is president and chief executive officer of the Hispanic Association on Corporate Responsibility (HACR), a national 501(c)(3) organization established in 1986 and based in Washington, DC. HACR's mission is to advance the inclusion of Hispanics in corporate America at a level commensurate with their economic contributions. Prior to joining HACR, Orta served in a variety of staff positions—external affairs, corporate foundation and government affair roles—at three Fortune 500 companies: Anheuser-Busch, Inc., Ford Motor Company, and Waste Management, Inc. Most recently he was selected by *Latino Leaders* magazine as one of the "101 Most Influential Leaders in the Latino Community."

Alison Kenney Paul leads the retail practice of Deloitte in the United States and she is a vice chairman. Paul has been president of the Network of Executive Women since October 2008 and has served the organization in numerous leadership positions. She served on NEW's executive committee as sponsorship chair, where she helped to double the number of the organization's national sponsors. She was also a co-chair and founder of the organization's Chicago regional group. Paul is responsible for overseeing one of the largest industry practices at Deloitte, which includes more than 1,400 professionals. She leads the development and oversees the implementation of key retail sector initiatives as well as working with senior management of the organization's leading clients. She is based in Chicago.

Carlos Santiago, president and chief strategist of Santiago Solutions Group, is a nationally recognized business strategist. He is known for his innovative branding, segmentation and ROI analytics. Carlos founded Santiago Solutions Group in 2000, developing proprietary econometric methodologies for growth opportunity analysis of the multicultural segments. Over the last 10 years, he has guided strategic growth, corporate, branding, engagement and social marketing strategies for a diverse group of organizations. Before branching out on his own, Carlos led Bell Atlantic-Verizon's diversity marketing for 8 years, where he oversaw P&L, brand strategy, service bundles, retail channels, customer service, direct response, promotions, and ROI with a $70M budget and 1,500 employees. Carlos is sought as a speaker on topics related to Hispanic consumer trends and preferences, in-culture marketing and communications, and growth in diversity markets.

Jessica Pantanini created the first Hispanic media optimizer, Millennium Media. In 2009, she testified before Congress to ensure that the single radio measurement tool had a sample frame that was truly representative of the market. Jessica testified on behalf of the Association of Hispanic Advertising Agencies (AHAA) demanding accreditation of Arbitron People Meter Methodology by the Media Ratings Council (MRC), in order to certify the accuracy of radio audience measurement. As COO, Jessica oversees the integration and quality standards for Bromley Communications. Her honors include being Hispanic Ad.com's, first recipient of the "Media

Planning Executive of the Year" award. She was also inducted into the American Marketing Association's (AMA) Godfathers of Hispanic Marketing Hall of Fame. Jessica serves as Treasurer of the Council for Research Excellence (CRE), and is the former President of AHAA.

Marie Quintana is senior vice president of PepsiCo multicultural sales, leading the sales activation of PepsiCo's ethnic programs. In this role, Marie drives the customer strategy for PepsiCo's multicultural markets, taking an integrated approach to align brands, retail activation programs and community initiatives. Marie's focus is a company-wide integration by working closely with multicultural and sales capability teams and she operates a Center of Excellence to drive best practices. Previously, Marie served in leadership sales roles with major corporations including IBM and Perot Systems.

Among her many affiliations, Marie serves on the board of the Network of Executive Women for Consumer Products and Retail; she Chairs the Corporate Advisory Board for Latina Style; and is on the board of PLAN of North Texas. She has been named one of the Top Women in Grocery by *Progressive Grocer,* and is featured in the book *The New Woman Rules.*

Gabriela Alcántara-Diaz recently started her own firm, GADMarketing Communications, based in Miami. A twenty-five year advertising veteran, Gabriela Alcántara-Diaz is recognized for managing agencies' multiple disciplines and cultivating client business strategic relationships. Her expertise includes ensuring sustainability and growth potential by interpreting analytics and insights into meaningful strategies that drive relevant positioning and thorough branding within the Hispanic marketplace. Throughout her career, Gabriela has been involved in brand and retail marketing; her clients benefit from her deep understanding of key industries including food, automotive, telecommunications and finance. She has been instrumental in developing ethnic store prototypes and retailer brand products.

Don Longo is editor-in-chief of *Convenience Store News*, *CSNews for the Single Store Owner*, and *Hispanic Retail 360* magazine. He also serves as editorial director for Stagnito Media. Don has covered retailing for almost 30 years as a reporter, editor and publisher. He co-founded and directs the content development for the Hispanic Retail 360 Conference, now in its eighth year. Previously, he spearheaded the editorial efforts at a variety of business publications covering the mass, drug, grocery, and specialty store retailing. Don received a Certificate of Merit from the Food Marketing Institute, and conducted face-to-face interviews with many prominent business personalities, including the late Sam Walton and Martha Stewart, among many others. He also is a member of the judging panel for the International Convenience Retailer of the Year award.

César M. Melgoza, founder and CEO of Geoscape is a leading innovator and thought-leader on business strategy, cultural insights and on the development of market intelligence systems and analytic services. After having fulfilled key roles at two Silicon Valley firms—Apple and Strategic Mapping—César founded Geoscape to create actionable insights for an increasingly diverse American and international marketplace. Mr. Melgoza has demonstrated remarkable elasticity during his lifetime—prior to his first birthday he and his family migrated from Mexico to a California farm labor camp where he lived until the age of nine and now he provides business counsel and technology to hundreds of senior corporate executives.

Douglas Darfield, senior vice president, multicultural measurement, Nielsen Media Research leads the Hispanic Services group and works closely with the general managers of the national and local business units. He also assumes a leadership position with regard to the company's Hispanic research functions and serves as Nielsen Media Research's industry representative.

Before joining Nielsen Media Research, Doug spent over 10 years as vice president and director of research for Univision, the Spanish-language television network. After leaving Univision, Doug was a research consultant for Televisa in Mexico City and director of network research for Hispanic Broadcasting Corp. Most recently, Doug served as chief strategic officer of EMC3, an online media exchange in Mexico City.

Roberto Orci's 30 years in marketing and advertising in Mexico, Canada, and the U.S. make him a leader in his field. He was a brand manager at Procter & Gamble (Mexico); VP management supervisor at Ogilvy & Mather in the U.S., Canada and Mexico; and until 2002, president of the fourth largest independent Hispanic Agency in the U.S., La Agencia de Orci. Prior to joining Acento Advertising where he is currently CEO, Roberto headed Orci Management Consulting, with a mission to guide companies in profitable business growth in the Hispanic market. He sits on the Board of Directors of Taproot Foundation, the Advisory Board of Cal State University's School of Business and the Advisory Board of the University of Arizona Terry Lundgren School of Retailing.

Lucia Ballas-Traynor joined CafeMom in 2011 as co-founder and to lead the creation of a new website aimed at Hispanic moms and named, Mamás Latinas. Social networking, community and culturally relevant content will be at the core of this new site. Prior to joining CafeMom, Lucia was publisher of *People en Español*, the largest selling Hispanic magazine in the U.S. Prior to that, she held executive roles at MTV Tr3r and IDT Corporation. A Hispanic marketing veteran, Lucia started her career in Hispanic television nearly 25 years ago at Univision where she held various positions in communications, marketing and sales and was named general manager of *Galavision*. Lucia has been was named a "Media All Star" by *Adweek's Marketing y Medios*, and was profiled in *The Hollywood Reporter's* "Latino Power 50" list.

Lee Vann founded Captura Group in 2001 with a vision for providing Hispanic interactive solutions that generate a quantifiable return on investment. Lee spearheads Captura Group's online strategy development practice, providing specific expertise in the areas of Hispanic in-language and in-culture research and strategy. Prior to founding Captura Group, Lee launched L90 Latino, the Hispanic division of the publicly traded internet advertising company L90. As the VP of L90 Latino, Lee developed and implemented U.S. Hispanic online marketing initiatives for several Fortune 500 companies. Prior to L90, Lee lived in Madrid, Spain and was the country manager for Quidel Corporation, a U.S.-based medical diagnostics company.

Martha Montoya is the owner and partner of three companies: Los Kitos Produce (farms, packing house, and fruit grower/operator), Los Kitos Entertainment (a syndicated cartoon strip/content provider) and *El Mundo Newspaper* (largest and oldest Hispanic newspaper in Washington State). Martha has forged relationships with corporate America, state and federal leaders to understand and bring to the table candid conversations to find solutions for the business position of minority owned businesses. Among other positions on local, state and national committees, she serves on the Executive Board of the United States Hispanic Chambers of Commerce and is the Head of the Membership Committee of the National Association of Hispanic Publications (NAHP).

Dr. Federico Subervi is professor and director of the Center for the Study of Latino Media & Markets at the School of Journalism and Mass Communication, Texas State University-San Marcos. Since the early 1980s, he has been conducting research, publishing and teaching on a broad range of issues related to the mass media and ethnic minorities, especially Latinos in the United States. He is the editor and an author of the book *The Mass Media and Latino Politics: Studies of U.S. Media Content, Campaign Strategies and Survey Research: 1984-2004* (NY: Routledge, 2008). In June 2011 he was elected as the first academic officer to the Board of Directors of the National Association of Hispanic Journalists. In January 2011, he started his term on the Board of Directors of the Latino Public Radio Consortium.

Carlos E. Garcia, senior vice president for Hispanic market research at Knowledge Networks and the founder of Garcia Research Associates is a highly respected leader and authority in Hispanic research, providing insights that have guided major business, marketing and advertising efforts in a variety of industries. As founder and the guiding force of Garcia Research Associates and the Cada Cabeza^SM online panel—both now part of Knowledge Networks—his clients have included industry leaders in packaged goods, health care, entertainment and financial services. Mr. Garcia's research experience ranges from new product and ad development to segmentation to deep-dive economic, political and brand equity studies.

Derene Allen, principal of Santiago Solutions Group (SSG), brings strategic and tactical expertise in Latin America, Caribbean and U.S. Hispanic markets. Ms. Allen's specialties include quantifying the efficiency and ROI of clients' investment in the Hispanic market. She has experience in financial and internet services, as well as database management and loyalty programs. Ms. Allen recently returned to SSG after a two year sabbatical managing a Social Enterprise, whose beneficiaries were low income Latinas. She is also an Adjunct Professor at the University of San Francisco teaching Multicultural Marketing and Social Entrepreneurship.

INDEX